FI

Christian love

Maurice Smith

23. 1. 1972.

Ashburnham

FIVE FIVE FIFTY-FIVE

by

MAURICE SMITH

CHRISTIAN LITERATURE CRUSADE
LONDON

CHRISTIAN LITERATURE CRUSADE
The Dean, Alresford, Hants.

U.S.A.
Box C, Fort Washington, Pennsylvania 19034.

AUSTRALIA
Box 91, Pennant Hills, N.S.W. 2120.

NEW ZEALAND
Box 1688, Auckland, C.1.

also in

Europe, Canada,
Central America, South America,
West Indies, Africa, India,
Indonesia, Far East

First Published 1969

Printed in Great Britain
by Richard Clay (The Chaucer Press), Ltd.,
Bungay, Suffolk

CONTENTS

CHAPTER		PAGE
	Acknowledgments	6
	Foreword	7
	Preface	9
1	A Birth Certificate	11
2	Churches and Chapels	31
3	Do Not Disturb	51
4	Dynamite	68
5	A Bid For Freedom	86
	A Final Word of Explanation	109

ACKNOWLEDGMENTS

MANY thanks are due to Ron and Shirley Wing who heard the voice of God and counselled me to write.

To Mrs. Dorrie Brooking of the Christian Literature Crusade, who gave immeasurable encouragement and spiritual help.

To Hugh Thompson who 'translated the book from the original English' (to use his own words).

And to my dear wife and family who readily agreed to such personal disclosures being made public so that others might be helped.

MAURICE SMITH

FOREWORD

I HAVE not met Maurice Smith, but a friend of his and mine suggested that he send me a copy of his manuscript. I found it vivid and intriguing, just because he does not try to be sophisticated or theological but gets straight down to honest personal experience and does not leave that one path. The personal always grips me. Novels may have their place, but I never get away from the uncomfortable feeling, 'This never really happened', 'Could it really have happened that way?' But to me a life story is life; and it need not be egotistical. This one is not. It moves straight on over hill and valley, and I don't feel Maurice has skipped anything that mattered, whether painful or humanly humiliating. It is a young story: not young in the sense of a teenage tale but of a man near enough to his young days to speak to this generation; and when it comes to taking us with him through his varied Christian experiences they are varied enough and spiritually dramatic enough, and plainly told enough to grip any hungry heart, and they seem just about to cover the span of God's dealings with 'the growth of a soul'. It does not mean that God takes everyone of us all those ways, nor that we must be stumbled by any compulsive drive to imitate. It is really an unfinished story, because Maurice's is very much an unfinished life; but I have no doubt that God will speak to readers' hearts, as He has to mine.

NORMAN P. GRUBB,
Worldwide Evangelization Crusade

PREFACE

SINCE my youth I have never been able to evade the question: Why am I here? The answer has unfolded to me in a number of clear-cut experiences, each of which has caused me considerable upheaval. Some of my friends urged me to publish an account of these intimate and drastic steps so that others might be helped. This unveiling of my private life may shock the reader, but these personal disclosures are necessary in order that others may realise that openly facing a problem is halfway to overcoming it. Vague generalisations would help no one.

It was difficult to know where to begin, as I had never written for publication before and had little idea of presentation. The Cotswolds?—India?—Egypt?—or right back in those early years among the back streets of London? Yes, right back there, to London, where so little of what was happening was consciously realised, but where so many of one's present attitudes and reactions had their breeding ground. I have tried to avoid exaggeration, but with the passage of time it is possible that some of the minor details are not entirely accurate. All the names are real, and so sometimes I have avoided using the surname to obscure identity and on occasions I have thought it best to omit names altogether.

This is essentially a book of experiences, so I have not developed the theological arguments concerning each crisis of my life. The reader may feel that many controversial issues have been raised, but should understand that I make no claim to have reached finality of thought.

In fact, some extreme conclusions expressed in earlier chapters had to be modified later in the book in the light of further experiences. So please stay with me to the end. No doubt in coming days further adjustment to my views will be necessary.

My life has been quite ordinary by general standards, and yet along life's way God has touched me in a series of very real encounters.

My prayer is that many such ordinary people will also discover the life that is worth while through these pages.

MAURICE SMITH

July 1968

CHAPTER I

A BIRTH CERTIFICATE

WE lived in a back street of North London. The lamp-posts were our cricket stumps and the front gardens, such as they were, made our camps and hiding-places. In the terraced house in the middle of a long row lived three families; we were not self-contained, and it was a crowded existence.

Mother and Father were so much older than I was and so much older than the parents of my friends. I always knew this, but the memory remains vivid because of a few special incidents.

There was the day when I was about ten or eleven years old. Dad had been angry with me about something and shouted: 'You won't always have us here to guide you!' I was injured by that remark and even today I can almost feel the hurt inside me as I walked slowly and thoughtfully back to school. Were they going to die? Would I soon be alone? How could I possibly manage without them? I had no brothers or sisters, and suddenly I felt very lonely. Somehow, too, I felt unsafe during those early years. Although I had auburn hair I was unable to live up to the epithet 'Ginger for pluck' and remember how scared I was of others at school in spite of my swaggering exterior. Dad had been a boxer at the Caledonian Baths in his early life and feared no one. 'The bigger they are, the heavier they fall' was his motto;

but it never seemed to work out like that for me.

Another day in my 'teen years I was talking to the Colonel of the local Army Cadet Corps; by this time I was the Sergeant-Major of this military-minded assortment of youth. Sixteen or seventeen years of age, a voice like a fog-horn and everyone was predicting a successful Army career ahead. The Colonel asked me if I had ever considered why my parents were so much older than the parents of the other lads. Well, frankly I hadn't; but now it began to be an issue with me.

There was plenty of time to think throughout those long nights when during the air-raids I patrolled the blacked-out streets with the Air Raid Precaution Service. It was quite exciting running messages from the local A.R.P. post to headquarters, and sometimes even from the bomb-site itself. Looking at the stars and listening to the drone of the bombers I began to ponder what life was all about.

A year or so later found me in the Army proper, with the war in Europe nearly at an end. I left the bomb-scarred streets of London and was soon a candidate for Officer Cadet School. Everything was going smoothly until one day the Adjutant made a determined request for a larger birth certificate than the one I had presented. He said this was not the original, and it seemed that my whole military future hung upon the production of this full-sized piece of paper. My parents were adamant that there was no other certificate and the Adjutant was equally adamant that there was. Then came the ultimatum—produce the original or return to my unit and forsake my promotion.

How well I remember the scene in that dark back

kitchen. It was there that Mother broke down and amidst her tears produced a full-sized document. It was headed boldly: Certificate of Adoption . . .

The world stood still during those long moments. It was quite a shock. Now I learned the story of how they had lost their own four children at birth and had taken me in as a baby. The intention had been that I should never know the truth.

I had been well and truly spoilt. How everything fits into place in retrospect! All my fears were sown in those early years: 'Be careful of the roads—you'll get run over.' . . . The fear of doctors and hospitals—'If you swallow a pip from that orange you're bound to get appendicitis, then you might develop peritonitis and even die.' . . . 'Be careful, don't walk under ladders; you'll have bad luck.' It was a realm of black cats, crossed knives and throwing salt over your shoulder. Thousands of little incidents moulded fear deep into my being, fear so real that I awoke often with nightmares. Even the clock ticking on the mantelpiece was to me a thousand marching men growing louder and nearer until they climbed the bed-post, and I could hold out no longer and a piercing scream would bring my parents running to the bedroom.

It all seems so silly now but it was real enough then, and all brought about by Mother's attempt to protect the one small life that had been entrusted into her care.

Ironically enough I never found the news of adoption affected my love for them at all. They were Mum and Dad to me, and it was as simple as that; but I did begin to wonder about one well-spoken aunt who was socially quite out of character with the family and seemed so interested in me.

It was about this time that I began to feel very guilty. Whereas they had given me a home and food and love, all I had given them was abuse and ingratitude. Several times I had demanded to know why they had ever bothered to have a child, as they kept on at me so. They must have been hurt very much during those teenage years when I roamed the streets with the gang and came home at all hours. 'You only eat and sleep here' was my mother's constant cry, and it was quite true.

. . . . .

What about religion during those early years? Well of course, there were times when I had tried to do as I was asked. I remember becoming a member of the local church choir for a year or so. I had quite a good voice, and even sang in St. Paul's Cathedral; but I could never read music and this hampered things a bit, for it was the choir pay that was the real attraction. It was all terminated rather suddenly when I was thrown out for laughing at something rude in one of the services. It had been deadly boring, I was glad to be out, and it left more time for the streets.

Father was a member of some sickness club or other at the Baptist Church and went briefly along on a Sunday afternoon to pay his weekly subscriptions; this was the only time he darkened the doors. For a little while I was a member of the Sunday School and a keen Cub and then a Boy Scout, which all had Church connections.

Was it in those early contacts that I learned the one (misquoted) verse of Scripture that was to haunt me through so many later years, 'He that hungers and thirsts after righteousness shall be filled'? I must have heard it somewhere.

. . . . .

Soon after my eighteenth birthday I was six thousand miles away from home, and childhood was like a dream. Within months I was commanding a company of Punjabi soldiers on the North west Frontier of India. What a mixture I was by this time—refusing to consider any branch of the service but front-line Infantry and scared stiff to have dental treatment. The Officers' Mess with a bearer (Indian waiter) behind each chair was a frightening experience for someone who had often eaten with newspaper as a table-cloth and had never dined anywhere but in the kitchen. The British officers all seemed so well educated, whereas I had left school at fourteen with grandiose ideas of becoming a newspaper reporter. However, I stretched a bit more and pretended to move easily in this new realm of batmen and bearers, sherry-parties, horse-riding and the social round of an Indian Army officer. I was happiest when roughing it on convoy in the hills, dodging the activities of fearless attacking tribesmen who seemed to enjoy a fight as much as I enjoyed a football match.

High in the rugged hills of the Frontier I became interested in Confirmation, although I have no idea where my appetite was whetted for anything spiritual. It was arranged for a senior-ranking officer to come and instruct me. Well, whatever it was he had, I certainly did not want it, and I determined that this was the end of religion for me; but in spite of myself I found that this was what I wanted to talk about. With a glass in one hand and a cigarette in the other, I would talk into the early hours with anyone so inclined. I was hungry and thirsty for something, but did not know what.

By this time I had two mothers. The out-of-place aunt began writing to me in India and the letters were scent-filled and romantic. In fact, they clearly passed the veil of decent communication, but they were very welcome to a soldier thousands of miles away from home. Finally I challenged her that she was my mother, and she replied that 'blood was thicker than water' and that I was bound to have found out some time. Actually, I did not find that blood was thicker than water, and all my deep feelings remained towards my parents by adoption.

All this time I had been faithfully corresponding with my local sweetheart, and on my only leave to England became engaged with typical haste. To me courtship was a serious thing and I could not become lightly involved with anyone, for everything to me was intense and of a black and white nature. This meant that I was now engaged to someone I did not know very well, for most of our contact was by letter. Still, I had no doubts that this was the one person I wanted to marry. During all this period of courtship and maternal confusion things had been happening in my Service life. The Indian Army had decided to dispense with most of the British officers, which brought a complete change of environment for me. I reverted to my parent Regiment, the Royal Fusiliers, which was then in Egypt. Before long the fast life of Cairo night-clubs had replaced any interest in religion that had arisen on the lonely Afghan Frontier.

When I landed back on Blighty shores for demobilisation I soon arranged a meeting with my new-found mother and discovered the moral background of her life was steeped in sex. It did not take a Sherlock Holmes to deduce that I was illegitimate. The traits of this immorality were, I knew, embedded deep in my own personality, and I wondered what life held for me. Would my life produce ruined homes and all the misery I could see written into the face of this woman of the world? There was a daughter, Peggy, my sister I supposed; but she was desperately ill and died about this time. She was very young, in her early twenties, and the whole house was filled with sin and tragedy. It seemed that Peggy died suddenly of 'stomach trouble' and I recall being plagued with the thoughts of abortion and other unpleasant imaginations. My mother had had serious operations, she told me, and this had curtailed her activities with men, which seemed to be a big issue at the time. I had considerable stomach pain myself and the fear of cancer soon took a grip on my mind; it was hard to think of anything else. A duodenal ulcer was diagnosed and coughing blood and rolling on the bedroom floor at night completely convinced me that I too would die young. Matters were not helped by the discovery of a shadow on a lung at the same time.

Life seemed pointless, and I remember driving as fast and as close to other cars as I could, half hoping there would be a smash and I would be out of it. I had neither the courage to take my own life, nor the thoughtfulness for others who might be involved in any accident that I should cause.

How disappointed my blood-mother had been that I turned up to meet her in sports jacket and flannels. It was evident that she had wanted to be on the arm of an Army officer and not some young fellow that never commanded a second glance. I was feeling sick inside and couldn't have cared less about anything, least of all the clothes I was wearing. In a public-house off Warren Street in the West End of London she worked overtime on me. I was doing everything wrong, it seemed. Her priorities were quite simple: I had to 'get on' now that I had some Service standing and to do this two things were necessary. First, I must become a Freemason as soon as possible; she could arrange that through men she knew. Secondly, I had to break off my engagement, as the girl, although nice enough, had no background and would soon drag me down to the gutter again.

Something in me rebelled at this idea of getting on by pulling strings, so I said plainly that I was going to get married at the earliest opportunity and was well able to look after my own career. Nevertheless, my return to 'the land fit for heroes to live in' began to be a bitter disappointment. My unskilled services were not in very great demand. No one seemed interested in the fact that I had chosen to be an Infantryman and I was told it would have been better if I had concentrated on 'a trade' during my Service career. The mercilessness of the business world struck me forcibly and as the first traits of leftish thinking entered my mind, for once in my life, I voted Socialist. But I soon returned to the 'Blues' with the conviction that the left-wing politicians were well-meaning but totally incompetent. How sweepingly audacious can youth be? Really the political scene did not interest me, and it was easier to settle quickly and finally for one party and then concentrate on more important matters in hand.

You see, I had developed expensive tastes and found the back streets far beneath my dignity. Money was the real problem, I suppose. The Army Pay Office had credited the pay of two Lieutenant Smiths into my account for some months. With typical frivolity and carelessness, I had spent them both. Now there was a large red-ink entry that was being demanded of me. Yes, money was a real problem and was soon to become critical.

Within two months of landing, and at the ripe old age of twenty-one, I was married at the same church that threw me out for unseemly laughter. How ironical that the same man who discharged me should now make advances to my wife-to-be during marriage instruction classes. For sure this did not encourage any religious pursuits that might have been lying dormant in my thinking. On the wedding day this man of Holy Orders took a resolute step back from the chancel steps; doubtless it was the double effect of seeing the young ruffian now resplendent in full military regalia—Sam Browne an' all—and the strong smell of drink which I had taken to fortify my courage.

So now, with the responsibilities of married life, I set out to face civilian life and climb out of the Five-Pounds-Ten-a-Week clerical rut. Salesmanship was the obvious attraction to someone of my outgoing personality and initiative. Remaining true to type, I studied furiously for a few months and without finishing the course set out to reach my ambition by experience. The ambition seems modest enough now, looking back over twenty years; but it was pretty formidable then. It was Fifteen-Hundred-a-Year by the age of thirty, a biggish house and a car. Not exactly Rockefeller stuff, but plenty to keep my talents occupied.

One of my many employers was engaged in some sort of preparations for the visit of Billy Graham to Harringay Arena in 1954. Americans did not appeal to me much at the time; it seemed they thought they had won the war, and who was this fellow coming over here to preach at us, anyway? This employer told me about the need for 'conversion', but I could not really grasp the idea. It was like one of several steps along the way and I feel somehow it was very important. I never visited the Crusade but I liked the clean-looking preacher's pictures, and he seemed like a real man who had the guts to preach a message that was not popular; but naturally I made all the usual remarks about emotionalism and mass hysteria.

We were selling memorial stones at the time and I had soon picked up the name of Tombstone Smith among my friends. Having had considerable success with the sale of stationery and soap, this more difficult speciality-type article offered greater scope for financial reward. Whereas before I had been persuading office managers and shop-owners, now I was in contact with members of the general public and every one of them bereaved. There was considerable inner conflict, for I wanted them to add a few inches on the headstone, to put up the cost, and yet I was conscious that they might be in need of the money. It was evident to me also, that 'poor old Joe' was worth the largest memorial on earth immediately after the funeral; but as the weeks progressed, the light of reality would dawn that he would not really mind very much and would rather the family spent the money on themselves. So if I could get on the scene before they stopped crying, the chances of a substantial order were much greater. It impressed me that my employer would not encourage an early visit although we lost business often through it, and it was another small pointer that made me think about religion.

After a year of dealing with the bereaved I'd had enough and, after several interviews, was fortunate to land a very promising position as an agent for a cattle food manufacturer. Here the tide really turned, for I was virtually self-employed and remuneration was generous and directly related to my efforts and abilities. Moving in quick succession from the Isle of Wight to Hastings, to the lovely Cotswold hills, now began my fourteen years' selling to farmers which soon brought my ambition in view and finally ended in Sales Management and the like—but I'm rushing too far ahead.

Soon I had realised my target in terms of income, home and vehicle. I even had some of my own pigs growing through to bacon weight, and the back streets of North London were far behind me now!

The only trouble was I had not found peace of mind. Don't ask me to explain why, but the same irritations that were with me in India and in Egypt and while struggling on Five-Pounds-Ten-a-Week were with me now, the same immoral thoughts and deeds, the same worrying disposition. I was tempted to just raise my sights and push on in the rat race. Instead, I did a bit of very elementary reasoning. *I* was the only common denominator in all these situations. Could the trouble be just *me*?

I had a loving wife and two fine children who were starting private school education, preparing for public school to avoid a repetition of my own unhappy council school years. Ambition was realised, but a void was within.

Mother by adoption had passed away by this time and Father was living with us, enjoying every minute of his last years in the countryside. It seemed that a glass of ale and a game of dominoes would satisfy him to the end; but I was getting desperate!

Surely our contacts in life are not by accident? One of my business colleagues was an Australian who had been a fighter pilot some years before. On a train journey to Crewe he gave me a clear exposition of what I now know to be 'the Gospel'. He told me that a perfect man named Jesus Christ had died upon a Cross two thousand years ago and had taken the punishment of the whole world. Furthermore, if I personally accepted that what he had done was because of *my* bad life, then somehow His blood—shed all that time ago—would wash away my guilt and give me peace.

This sounded like good news to me, but I was unable to accept it. How could I be sure that it would work? I did not want to get wrapped up in some particular religious school of opinion, for it was the Truth I was after and was determined not to make a mistake after eight years of seeking. This seemed the only realm in which I was unprepared to make a hurried decision.

When we arrived at Crewe I forsook my religious friend for the company of the more socially acceptable and missed tragedy by a hairbreadth. Everyone seemed to be like dogs that had been let off the lead in a park. Most of the men had not been away from home since the war, and soon parties and dates were fixed with every available female in the hotel, and even on the streets. Very soon I was involved in something I knew would not turn out right for a married man and yet I did not have the courage to break out of it. Then, as I was leaving the dinner table, this same Australian gave me an invitation to a religious meeting and I jumped at it, as a means of escape. Running upstairs I ripped off my green bow-tie, put on something more sober and stepped out to a not-very-exciting little hall with bench-type seats gathered into the four sides of a square. They all sat round and talked and sang, but it was way beyond my understanding. My friend was obviously able to take part on his first visit and as he talked it seemed to me he knew God in some personal way.

How well I recall that same night back in the hotel bedroom. My room-mate was filled with remorse at having been so unfaithful to his wife. He had taken my place in the party and I felt sort of reprieved. I went to sleep hours later after much thought.

By this time I had learned one more quotation from the Bible. The Australian said emphatically, 'Seek, and ye *shall* find.' He said if I were really earnest and honest, then I would discover the truth, and he refused to discuss it any more.

Back in the village some time later a seemingly small incident had tremendous effect upon the whole course of my life. We were seated in the local inn. A village Football Club Committee was in progress and the large bare table was covered with pint jugs and fixture lists. We were selecting a list of likely Vice-Presidents from whom we could extract ten and sixpence, for the dubious privilege of having their names on the fixture cards. Who would approach the Rector? Well, no one fancied that job; after all, he was quite likely to ask some sticky question such as, 'We haven't seen you in church lately, have we?'—or something equally hard to answer without telling the offensive truth. The committee were unanimous—it was obviously my job. Was I not the Secretary and had I not got an Athletic Club background? The Rector was, they pointed out, an old Oxford Athletics Blue, and it would be easy to make contact.

It was a May evening. The Cotswold stone rectory looked cold and uninviting as I walked slowly towards it. The steps were steep, I noticed. Right down in the bottom of my being I sensed that this subscription-collecting mission was important. Before long I was on my way out with a cheque for half a guinea and his willing agreement to be a Vice-President.

'*Is everything all right with your soul?*' The direct nature of the question took me aback. I stopped halfway down the steps. 'No, it isn't,' I stammered, and we were soon back inside. This time we made for the leather-bound study, not the drawing-room; it was obvious he meant business. Soon I was confronted again with the claims of a Saviour who had died to bring forgiveness of sins and could meet the need of my unfulfilled life.

A railway carriage and a study; an Australian pilot and an English country Rector; but the same message, the same message I had so vaguely understood from the director of a tombstone business in North London.

Somehow I wanted this message, and yet I could not bring myself to kneel down there in the study and admit my need, as he was suggesting. Just like my Australian friend, the Rector said I knew enough and now the decision was up to me. It seemed that I was at a crossroads. Would I surrender my whole life to God or continue to run my own affairs?

What a fool I would feel kneeling down there in confession. No, it was more than that; perhaps I was still not quite sure that this was what I was after. Would it work? Could such a simple receiving of what someone else had done really set *me* free? Would it answer *all* the problems of my tangled life? Surely I would have to earn my place in heaven—if there were such a place—for it seemed too good to be true, that all I had to do was trust this other man's death for *my* guilt, and anyway, I did not feel particularly guilty now! But I did have a deep sense of need.

Besides, what about the Pygmies? For some reason I always kept these midget men in reserve. They were my last resort against accepting this message of forgiveness through believing. It may seem strange, but it was the one big thing I kept getting stuck on. How about all the people who had never heard about this free pardon and had died? Surely God could not be so unfair as to forgive those who had heard while He condemned these midget men? Don't ask me why it was the Pygmies I was so concerned about. No doubt if this Pygmy-argument had been settled, then I would have produced another one. It was rather like a game of skittles—I'll stand 'em up and you knock 'em down. Perhaps God was going to give me some answers on the other side of my acceptance by faith? I was getting dangerously near to surrender, but all I knew was that I was in desperate need of a personal answer and so, reverently, the Pygmies would have to wait!

Through my mind went all the times I had stood staring into space wondering if it were all a dream, wondering if I were really here at all, pinching myself when no one was around as if to make sure that I was solid. If there were such a thing as matter, then it must have started somewhere, and soon I was back to the old chestnut, Who made God? The times my simple mind wound its laborious way back to that original speck of dust and where that had come from! Wrestling with infinite problems with a very finite mind proved fruitless; it seemed that these things had got to be spiritually discerned rather than figured out or heaven was going to be full of University professors.

No! I would not accept just like that. It must be more difficult and so I said 'good night' to the Vicar (I could never get used to calling him Rector) and strode off up the village street. It was quite late now.

The previous encounter with the Rector had been on my 'trial run' at his church when I made my home in the village, and I pondered over this. The place had been nearly empty and there were rows of vacant pews; however, I had the misfortune to sit in someone else's seat. The dear lady was so upset that she nearly sat on my lap throughout the service. I felt sure that if there were such a place as heaven she was not going to make it, and if she did, then I didn't particularly want to share it with her. The whole set-up seemed plain wrong and yet this strange message, that I could have a new life, had affected me very much. Even if the parishioners did not seem to be enjoying this free and happy existence, was that any reason for me to miss out on it? 'Stop looking around and start looking up,' the Rector had said.

From all this I had learned my third verse of Scripture. It was Revelation three, verse twenty, although I did not know that at the time. 'Behold, I stand at the door, and knock: if any man hear my voice, and open the door, I will come in . . . ' *Any man!*

Straight up the street, into the house, through the downstairs rooms, up to my bedroom and down on my knees. Oh, I did so want peace. I was tired of being so irritable, tired of always threatening to take my life, which had no meaning, tired of unclean thoughts and habits. I wanted to be right inside, to be clean, to have a good conscience.

Well, I prayed . . . what I would not do before a witness such a short while ago, I did now. It went something like this: 'I'm not sure about all this, but somehow I believe You are God and if this verse that I have learned is really true, will You come in now and change my life?' Not much faith there, I fear, but it was real and it was honest.

As I rose and came down the stairs I knew something had happened. It seemed that a voice, not exactly audible, was telling me not to mention this transaction to anyone; it must be kept dark. I had no idea how important it was for me to tell someone; that the Bible teaches, 'If you confess with your mouth the Lord Jesus . . . you shall be saved,' but someone else knew how important it was. This voice was not of God—of that I was sure—and within a few moments of accepting Jesus Christ as my Saviour personally I had encountered opposition from powers of darkness. I knew the devil was real straightaway. However, that which is in the heart of a man comes out at the mouth and something had certainly happened inside me. There was an immediate sense of well-being; a peace which could not be explained on a human level, for all the circumstances around me were the same. It was extraordinary, for I seemed now to know God personally all of a sudden; a barrier had been removed and I was in touch.

Within days of my conversion I wanted to own a Bible. All through the years of discussion I never once considered actually purchasing a Bible. Now I hot-footed off to Chipping Norton with the excitement of a young child after a new bike. The man in the shop seemed to understand exactly how I felt and was just like a brother to me; it was obvious to me that he knew my God too. I had never had a brother and the new family affection was quite a lovely experience. The antequated wording of the standard version seemed ridiculous to me in the twentieth century, all those 'thees' and 'thous'! I was looking for something up to date and bought a modern translation and was soon back home underlining verses that were so meaningful to me. There seemed to be an actual new life inside me that wanted food and could find satisfaction nowhere else but in the words of this book, which had suddenly become my richest treasure.

I was so happy. In the evening my wife would sit and watch the television, and I would sit just reading this Bible for hours. Not quite sure what had happened, I soon found myself telling everyone how marvellous this experience was and saying that they could have it too. After all, it was a free gift, and it was now apparent to me that many other folk were also in great need. Strangely enough, few seemed to want this free gift. I remember feeling like a man who had discovered the sure cure for cancer and no one wanted to know.

'Some seed fell in good ground and it grew . . . ' My wife, Eileen, was one of the first to come into this wonderful new experience with God, although in quite a different way from me. Eileen had always been of a placid temperament, whereas I had been impetuous and full of worries. The 'duodenal' that had been mine so young was not likely ever to come her way. Come to think of it, she has always been remarkably fit. While I have been panicking over suspected tuberculosis, admitted to hospitals for tonsils, appendix and two hernias, she has kept clear of all troubles. Even the deliverance of children was effected with the minimum of fuss; for one morning I was presented with a cup of tea and the cool remark that a child would soon be arriving. Having had one experience of only just getting to hospital in time, I was soon up and driving furiously through the town. A policeman took out his book as we passed, but it was no time to stop and explain. Within a short time we had a new baby daughter.

Eileen could take everything in her stride, it seemed, and all the time that I was fretting over what was going to happen to us when we died, she would phlegmatically reply, 'We'll face that when it comes, dear.'

What could so affect my wife that could cause her to desire Christian conversion? It would be false humility to deny that it was the obvious change in my own life. When I had asked Jesus Christ to come into my life and opened the door that May evening, He had come in. Not bodily, but His Spirit had come in and was expressing Himself in strange ways. I found this new life in me wanted to wash up dishes and do other chores that had been irksome to me before. Finally, about nine months after my own experience, my wife came to know the Lord personally and God was beginning to answer my prayers and those of the little group that met so unobtrusively in the rectory drawing-room once a week.

Everything seemed new. Now I understood what Jesus meant when He said to that very religious man so long ago: 'You must be born again.' That was what had happened to me; it was none other than a new birth. Now I had the most wonderful Birth Certificate—God was my Father and my name was written in heaven.

Years of seeking had ended on May the Fifth, Nineteen Fifty-Five, when a seed that was planted in my heart broke out and began to grow. Jesus said, 'The seed is the Word,' and I had received His Word and that day of receiving is still the most memorable day of my life. I have always had a bad memory and I have often thought that God, who knows everything, took note of that and caused my second birthday to be 5.5.'55 so that I would never forget—as if I ever could!

CHAPTER II

CHURCHES AND CHAPELS

'You don't have to go to church to be a Christian!' Along with most other people I had expressed these sentiments often enough. Now I had to take note of the surprising fact that this new life which I had received was not content to live alone. To be along with others who had also experienced a personal transaction with God became essential to me, and so I began attending a weekly Bible study and prayer group down at the rectory. It would be dishonest to say I enjoyed it very much; but I couldn't stay away. We used to sit round the fire in the lounge and the Rector would explain a passage to us, and then there would be a short discussion. Afterwards, kneeling down together, we used to pray out loud, one after the other, going round the half-circle. This was an awful ordeal to me, for I had never said prayers in my life and was not very good at it. I said I would not continue to come if they persisted with this consecutive praying, in which you either had to join, or be terribly conspicuous by your silence when it came around to your turn. They agreed to stop it for my sake. No sooner had they stopped it than I felt we were losing something very valuable and asked for it to start again!

I wanted to get down to business (whatever that meant) and this highly respectable group of Church of England folk seemed unlikely to turn the world upside down. It seemed to me that what I had found was so emancipating that everyone ought to know immediately; but my enthusiasm was outrunning my understanding of what had happened and probably my zealous testimony would never survive any logical opposition unless I received some sound teaching.

Gradually I began to conform to the ideas being put to me by the experts at the rectory, although I must admit I was uneasy within; there was some kind of Witness down inside me that did not seem to be able to agree with some of the religious views being put to me. It was a kind of Inner Voice I now had that had not been there before; but I had not learned to respect the voice, and it was not very clear really. Perhaps I had to tune up my inner hearing?

Take the matter of infant baptism, for instance. Well, I had never been 'done' as a child and so the suggestion was made that I ought to be christened now—at twenty-eight years of age this was—and then be confirmed straight away. Something in me was saying 'No', but I could not be sure; after all, this good man of God had been right about my needing to receive God in a personal way. He said I would find peace and I had, so perhaps he was right about this also. In addition to this, I did not really want to displease him if I could possibly help it, for he had been such a help to me. In all this confusion I went ahead with the necessary classes, but they did not deeply convince me. In spite of all this my wife and I agreed to go through it all together.

We needed a couple of god-parents and, in a circle that is not God-fearing, serious-minded god-parents are not easy to come by. Our close friends from North

London, Ronnie and Shirley, were very happy to oblige. They were five years our junior and still seeking reality for themselves; but this did not seem to bar them, for they had unknowingly become eligible when they were babies.

What a disappointment that day was to prove for both my wife and me. There we were gathered in the morning around the font in the village church, listening to words that were beautifully phrased but totally lifeless to both of us. Then, in the evening we all went off to a nearby town to await the Bishop. Surrounded by many giggling girls, who were all in white, we felt quite out of place. Everything to us was deadly serious, but to these young ladies it all seemed so frivolous. We were longing to go right on with God, and perhaps they were too, but it did not show much in their demeanour. Why didn't the Bishop talk more about Jesus Christ, I wondered? How could these religious men make so complicated and intellectual something so simple. I stood meditating. As far as I could ascertain, Jesus had always got on fine with the common folk, whereas this man seemed remote from me and I became rather engrossed in examining the unusual clothes he was wearing. Was all this in the Bible, I began to wonder? Was I beginning to be trapped into a system?—perhaps after all those years I had been caught. I was beginning to conform and deep down within I felt I was making a mistake.

How grateful I was to one dear soul who came to my aid on the way out of the church. She must have seen how downcast and perplexed I looked, as she stopped me in the porch and said, 'Don't worry, Maurice, that's not it!' She encouraged me to believe that God knew my heart's longing and would lead me in a right path as time went by. I had always liked this youngish woman with a boyish complexion. She was a schoolteacher and came along to the rectory group. It was so evident that her Christianity was much more personal than that of most other people. Right back there, I remember too how she was devoid of the outsized hat that seemed part of the religious uniform of so many of our dear ladies. Isn't it strange how little things like that strike you so forcibly? In a nutshell, she seemed human and free. This timely word, whispered in my ear, was like oil on a rough sea to me.

Everyone was very understanding with me, for I must have been pretty unbearable to them in those early days. I had not grown very far in Christian grace and many things puzzled me and I said so. Above all, I could not fathom why the message which had been so challenging to me had not found its place in the preaching from the pulpit. Maybe it had and I couldn't recognise it, but it certainly lacked the forthrightness and power of those staccato words on the steep stone steps.

Something else, much more personal, was bothering me too. It was the conviction of my wrongdoing. The old Bible word Sin was beginning to mean something to me now. Things were being seen in a different light altogether, for instead of worrying how *I* felt and what happened to *me*, I was starting to consider how my behaviour affected others. To take an extreme case: what about the men I had killed?—men who had been shot down under my orders as they raided our desert camp and stole the army stores. The memory of collecting their dead bodies and loading them in the back of a fifteen-hundredweight truck was quite vivid to me now. I remembered how I had to help the Sergeant load them myself, for some of the lads felt so sick. Could all this be right? As my new religious friends and I talked it became obvious that mortal combat did not seem to be so horrific to them as it had become to me. I felt clearly that I would not be able to put my finger round a trigger again, for I wanted to live at peace with all men, and even be able to offer them the other cheek to smite if they had hit one side already. The Rector quoted the Scriptures about Jesus going into the temple, overturning the money-lenders' tables and making a whip and using it to clear His Father's house of the thieves. I counter-quoted my Scripture, which I had found in my new treasure book, and which said, 'If my kingdom were of this world, then would my servants fight!' Did this mean that my Christian life was going to hold complications? I was not a very clever kind of fellow and knew I would never be able to sort out right from wrong on this comparative-scripture basis. The peace in my heart was wonderful, but how was I going to stay on this strait and narrow pathway? There were now so many voices, religious voices too, telling me to believe so many different things. I was grateful for this still, small inner voice, which had come with my conversion experience. Somehow I could recognise it as the Truth and again, somehow, knew the difference between this voice and the one that had told me to keep quiet as I came down the stairs from my encounter with God. It is difficult to describe a voice; much easier to describe a person. 'My sheep know my voice,' the Bible says, and I knew I was going to have to listen carefully to this inner registration as well as read the words of the Bible. I was going to have to set aside all preconceived ideas too and let God rule in everything, else there was no point in His telling me things if I were not going to accept them; so I reasoned.

How well I remember the night that the group studied the passage in which the great apostle Paul stated that he was the least of all the saints. I said outright that the man was a hypocrite, for he was obviously one of the greatest of saints and was indulging in false humility. It is with gratitude that I think of the long-suffering of those dear folk with me. Knowing nothing of the way God could so deal with a man that he could be used so mightily as Paul and yet be genuinely convinced of his unworthiness, I was ever ready to voice my opinion on all these matters. Don't you think God was merciful and gracious to bother with me at all? I do. Deep down underneath all this outward brazenness was a heart that wanted nothing less than reality and I suppose He must have given me that, too, when I come to think of it.

Have you ever had anything to do with a Parochial Church Council meeting? Well, I do hope your experience was more pleasant than mine. It was grim. The dear Rector had such a job to make sure everyone was kept happy; at least, that is how it appeared to me. I was just bursting at the seams to stand up and get things moving, but did not know how to without causing offence. It was all so frustrating and I just felt as though I had got caught up with an old ladies' sewing class. Nothing, it seemed to me, could be farther removed from the sort of meeting at which I would have found those rugged disciples of Jesus so long ago. It was on the way out that the headmaster of a local Public School drew me aside in the dark village street—people seemed to feel guided to draw me aside after meetings to make sure I did not throw in the sponge! This particular man had been a missionary, I was told, and he certainly had a ring of authority about him as he spoke to me that night. 'If you are ever called to preach, young man, remember these words that the Lord said to Peter: "Feed My sheep." He did not say, "Tickle the ears of the goats."' And with that he walked off into the night. It had been said with a twinkle in the eyes, but had made an indelible impression on my mind. I knew it was from God, a voice not this time from within but from without.

I realised that the Man I was following never persuaded His followers to stay with Him, but made it difficult by saying it would cost them everything to be His disciples. He said to them once, 'Will you also go away?' and they had replied, 'To whom can we go? You have the words of eternal life.' So it was with me, and I purposed never to offer a popular message if ever I were privileged to preach; although at that time, preaching for me seemed quite unlikely.

My new friend, the Rector, was soon off to fill a University post in Ireland, and I was amazed when he said God had sent him to that village that I might become a Christian. He had been there eight years, but now had a sense of release and was able to leave. I had found new life and would ever be grateful that he had stayed and served, even though at times he had wondered at the lack of fruit—grateful especially for his faithfulness on that May night when he had spoken so directly and clearly to my soul.

Soon I was away too, but not for very spiritual reasons, I'm afraid. There was a real dearth of athletic facilities in that Cotswold agricultural district and I longed for the cinders again. It had been so long since I had heard the sound of a starter's gun or the ring of the bell that said so ominously, 'One lap to go.' Not that I was very special as a performer, but the sport had got into my blood, or at least I thought it had. There was a track at Iffley Road, Oxford, which was used by the University. It was too many miles from my village to offer much and so I had kept reasonably fit by jogging the roads and a few laps of the football pitch. The night Roger Bannister broke the Four-Minute Mile at Iffley I had tossed over in my mind the idea of making the journey but had decided against it. The conditions were unfavourable and he would never do it, anyway! So I stayed home and missed the biggest thrill you could have offered me at that time. Now I would move South, where the tracks were, and follow the sport again. It was ironic that the only available business agency was way down in the South-East and I arrived only to find a complete lack of sporting facilities again! I had a couple of outings with a nearby Athletic Club and toyed with the idea of starting a more local club, but other things took a hold on me.

Down in the picturesque village, where I had made my new home, I sought to continue my spiritual life, but something had gone wrong. I was beginning to meet the snags!

Of course the first port of call was the vicarage, only to find a garden party was in progress. Once again I had that awful feeling of being out of place, just like I had felt at the church council meeting, only this time it was greatly intensified. There was such an artificial atmosphere, rather like a cocktail party it seemed to me, as I tried hard to listen to the idle chatter. I began to feel a bit sick, not this time by my Mother's unveiled suggestions as to how I should get on in life, but by an overshadowing of unreality—of play-acting. Would I like to look over the vicarage which had been given by the parishioners in appreciation of services rendered? No, I would not! Well, that was not very polite, was it? But again as before my conversion, I was getting to the end of my tether. This time I was not seeking for real peace of mind—I had found that—but for real Christian friendship. Why could I not get close to these people? They seemed so pious, so ultra-respectable and I quite honestly preferred most non-church-goers to my new associates. Here was a fine mess to be in; it seemed just like coming out of the frying-pan into the fire.

As I listened to the sermons week by week I realised this was what the apostle Paul had called 'another gospel'. It did not speak of an offering once made by Jesus, which meant you could be made right with God through faith alone. This message said, in no uncertain terms, that if you did the best you could in this life, then you would make heaven in the next. I knew that my best was so despicable that there was only one place in which that could land me!

I tried hard to persuade the Vicar to have a Bible study or a prayer time in order that together we might discover the Truth; but, in spite of endless promises, it never materialised and was obviously not wanted. Sunday services were all that really mattered, it seemed, and these were dead as a dodo to me. Those sermons! Completely lacking in conviction and life. (One day I was convinced the dear man had turned over two pages at once without noticing it.) The message brought on Youth Sunday by a local councillor, to a group of scouts and guides, was so much in opposition to what the Bible taught that I almost stood up and made a public protest right there in the church. Discretion (or was it fear?) just won the day, and I parted company with a Gospel-rejecting local Church of England to see what the Methodists had to offer.

The Methodists caught me out with two collections in the one service and, having put my collection money in the first time round, I was embarrassed at the repeat performance. A special collection for needy believers seemed right according to the New Testament, but I sensed that it would have been better to have an unobtrusive box or bag somewhere, so that you would not look such a meanie if you could not, or did not want to, participate. Of course with a deft move of the hand you could pretend to subscribe, I suppose, for I remember as boys that some used to boast they could take more out than they put in; but I had never been much of a one for stealing—except for a few sweets from the corner shop or a bar of soap from Woolworths, I had kept clear of this area of crime. (Don't ask why a small boy should steal toilet soap, and then be so sure that he would be found out that it was finally pushed down a drain!) On this occasion of the double collection I just apologised rather awkwardly and passed the bag along.

These people seemed much friendlier than any church-goers I had met up to now. They even wanted to talk about the things of God as well as matters concerning homes and children. The first week there, we were invited home to tea and I began to wonder, 'Is this what I've been looking for?' Very soon I was in real trouble and all over the matter of preaching which had been mentioned to me by the public school headmaster after the Cotswold church council meeting. The lay minister very soon recognised that I was keen and not just desirous of filling a pew-space for the next forty years. It was suggested immediately that I ought to become a local preacher, although I said that I was by no means ready yet. Then I was told, this was quite true; but by the time I had been trained in the doctrines of John Wesley and passed some sort of examination that I would be ready to travel the Circuit, as they called it. A senior minister was brought in, I remember, to put all this over to me.

The whole thing just failed to register with me. That Inner Witness down inside was again at work. It told me that this was not right. It was John Wesley's own father, I believe, who was so strong on this matter of the Inner Witness. It is reported that on his death-bed he said, 'The Inner Witness, John—the proof of Christianity,' or something very similar. Certainly from the time when I accepted Jesus Christ as my Lord to run my life, I have had such an inner sense of direction. Sometimes it is not always as clear as I would like and then there seems a real need to be very still, and not to make hurried decisions, or be forced into decisions by others.

'Could I just preach from the Bible?' I asked. I suggested that if they did not agree with what I said, then they could call out, or discuss it with me afterwards, as they did with Wesley. After all, he got his inspiration from God and cut right across the previous traditions of the religious folk. Might it not be that God would reveal to me new areas of truth that would cut right against the traditions that men had built around John Wesley? Well, these views did not exactly place me at the top of the popularity poll and it was clearly, but nicely, pointed out that either I would have to do things their way (to conform to the Nonconformists) or not preach at all. So, before I got too enmeshed I left, saying I must find a spiritual home where I felt God was actually moving today, as it seemed to me that the power that had so evidently been present in the beginnings of Methodism was missing now. Furthermore, and much more important, there did not seem the liberty to allow God to do a new work and bring the power back.

About this time, still within a year of my bedside conversion, I was drawn to investigate the claims of an organisation called Toc H. This movement, it seems, was started in the First World War, over the other side, at Poperinghe. Toc H, I soon learned, was signalling language for T.H. which in turn stood for Talbot House, the three-storey house where the work first began. Soldiers were brought in downstairs, tired with the rigours of battle and given Char and Wads, and later encouraged upstairs to talk over spiritual needs. Right up the top there was a chapel, into which they were brought, if the desire for worship was there. It was an approach through service. The symbol was an eastern oil lamp and the motto taken from the fifth chapter of Matthew's Gospel: 'Let your light so shine before men, that they may see your good works, and glorify your

Father which is in heaven.' So good works had become the prime object. We did a lot of talking about doing a lot of jobs; but I began to realise that with monotonous regularity the same few actually turned up to do the jobs. They were very keen for me to join. (Why does everyone want you to join something?) Spiritually they encouraged anyone to come and teach, and so I took full opportunity to preach the Gospel, particularly showing that good works would not get you to heaven but that it was absolutely essential to trust in the punishment that Jesus took for our sins. It was suggested at one time that I would make a good Pilot—the fellow responsible for the spiritual side of things—while the Chairman and Secretary had the overall government. I sought to explain that we all ought to be spiritual men and that prayer and the study of God's Word were for every one of us. I must have seemed quite eccentric to some, I suppose. This lamp, which was their symbol, seemed to lack oil to me and was in danger of going out. Was this one more case of man trying to keep something going that God had spontaneously started to meet the need of those fighting-men in the front line? That's how it began to seem to me, the old round of recruiting drives and the like. Once again, far removed from the early Church power that I longed to see flowing again.

As I have remarked earlier, these searchings are not in vain. It was a Toc H man who stopped me one day on the street with a problem. He was the headmaster-elect of a school in Africa, or something like that, and the problems connected with the move were right on top of him. As he unburdened himself to me, I began to point him to the One Man that I knew could help him and take the load from off his back. If He had met me in all my need, then I knew He could do the same for Les. My counsel was quite clearly and honestly rejected with the rejoinder that only that very same morning he had received a letter from someone very much like me. It was an invitation to a meeting from a local schoolmaster who, according to Les, was always talking about Jesus Christ in the same personal way that I was. Still longing for close friendship with kindred souls, I soon relieved him of the invitation to what was simply termed a Christian Meeting. I made my way along—what would I find this time?

Twenty or thirty people gathered together in a rather shabby hired hall with an Irishman in front preaching his heart out. 'Be it unto me according to thy word,' was his message; the words so willingly spoken by Mary when the angel came and said she would conceive and bear a child, although she was not married! I was gripped by the preaching, for there was power here and I was helped—sort of 'built up inside' is how I would explain it, and no ministry before had had this effect. It seemed as if I grew a little during the meeting.

Soon I learned that these people were attending different churches and had quite different backgrounds. They came together, they said, because they were hungry for some spiritual food which they were not getting at their various places of worship. They had no doctrinal basis for meeting and said that nothing held them together except the common life they all shared by virtue of their personal encounters with God. I could hardly believe it. Many of my questions began to be answered at this fortnightly meeting. From the Scriptures I learned how we were all 'one in Christ Jesus'—how drawing up rules and regulations could only keep us apart rather than draw us together—how cliques were so easily formed around special aspects of truth instead of all going on together—that the church consisted of people (what the New Testament called Living Stones) and had nothing to do with buildings—the church was not a place but a people. All this really rang my bell and the Inner Witness was giving full approval.

My Sunday church-going activities I had transferred from the Methodists to the Baptists by this time, and it was while attending here that I had encountered the group which met in the little hired hall. The nearest Baptist chapel was in a village two miles away from my home and it was there that I went regularly. Immediately I realised that the messages from the pulpit were far more clearly related to what I found in the Bible than anything I had heard up to date in a church building. I did not want to separate from them because I knew they were believers and I could recognise truth as far as I could discern. Particularly did I like the fact that there were some young people who had a real love for God, and I had never found any young people in the church before. There were only children who *had* to go, and elderly people who perhaps were thinking about the end of the journey; or so I reasoned. The middle group of young people were conspicuously missing from most places I had visited.

What a grievous disappointment lay ahead of me. One Sunday the Minister announced a church meeting during the week. It seemed an important meeting and I wanted to go along and take my share of responsibility. 'See you there, Jack,' I called to my new Baptist friend. His face dropped. 'Not you, Maurice,' he replied, 'it's only for members.' I protested that I was a member. That there was only one church and I had been born by a new-birth experience into that; that I was one with every other believer who had come to know Christ. I pointed out, as best I could, that the Bible spoke of 'the Church which is His (Jesus') body', and that we were all members of the body just like members of the human body. We were either in it and could not leave it, or we were not in it. It seemed that this was quite understood, but it was the Baptist Church they were talking about. Now the light fully dawned—'You've got a church all of your own!' I exclaimed. I just could not get across to him that there was only one Church, that there was no Baptist Church, Methodist Church, Anglican Church, Roman Church, Pentecostal Church, Congregational Church, End-Time Church or any other *kind* of church. All believers were one and were never meant to major on any one aspect of doctrine and form up around it. I could quite see that most of these sects had, at some time, represented some vital aspect of recovered truth but our God was marching on and He did not expect us to pitch our tent short of the full end. The Baptist Hymnal, I pointed out, said: 'The Lord has yet more light and truth to show forth from His word!' So on my questing way I went.

The Church is not an organisation but a body of people who have Christ's Life in them. They do not need special buildings to meet in for they themselves are the Church. This truth, which it seemed had been hidden for so long from many, began to grip me as I read my

Bible and regularly attended the fortnightly meeting in the hall in the city. The Irishman I learned had, in fact, been a Baptist minister but had to leave the organisation, because of his marching forward. One Sunday, for instance, he had had no message from God for the people. Now it would have been easy with his alert mind to think one up; but he was too real to do such a thing. When he learned that one of the other members had something to say that he felt was from God, he opened his pulpit readily. This action, which apparently upset so many, seemed to me like a breath of freedom that should be welcomed rather than suppressed, if we were ever to get back to that early Church authority and power.

There were small groups of people around the countryside I discovered who seemed to agree with what I was saying. These little groups that I had found were called 'the Brethren' by other people although they did not want to be called anything themselves. There seemed to be different groups of them which people called 'Open Brethren' and 'Exclusive Brethren' and this latter group seemed to have numerous divisions, like the 'Kelly Brethren' and the 'Raven Brethren'; these I guessed to be the names of prominent men. Although the folk I met claimed that there was no division, it seemed to me that there was a very strong inference that 'We are the true Church.' Everything centred around what was 'said' in the Bible and there was so little evidence of the spontaneous joy that I had found, the glorious liberty and lack of bondage in being a Christian. Although they had nothing written down regarding laws and regulations, whenever we talked I sensed a kind of legality, or a rigidness, in so many. No doubt they had real light on many things, but oh, the lack of vitality! Was this how that early church pioneered the Gospel? I wondered if many of these dear folk had all the teaching about a new experience with Jesus Christ but, by virtue of being sons of fathers who believed, had failed to have this tremendous transaction themselves.

Somehow the doctrine of separation from the world that these friends were expounding to me seemed to be a real aggravation to my Inner Witness, and it did not tie up at all with what I could see of the life of Jesus in the Bible. He loved to be among the outsiders and to eat and to drink with them. He also had a way with common folk that I noticed was missing from many of these devout people. Being newly converted to Christianity, I was very sensitive to things which concerned those who did not go to church. The A.A. badge on my car was one thing that caused great concern. How could I be in an association with others who might be doing all sorts of evil things? one man asked me bluntly. 'Be ye not unequally yoked together with unbelievers' was the text upon which this apparent revelation was hung. This letter-of-the-law application really did alarm me, for I realised that if I followed this principle to its logical conclusions I was going to need a sect all of my own before long. When we talked together, Scripture was made to be a divisive thing whereas all the time my heart was being enlarged, by the Holy Spirit within me, to reach out in friendship towards all men. I was quickly learning that 'The written law brings death, but the Spirit gives life.' Again I asked more questions of myself. Could these earnest people really have the Holy Spirit's inner witness? If so, was He being allowed to govern or were clever men getting their minds to work on the divine Book, which needed the Spirit of God as the interpreter?

This church-going was proving quite a problem after all, so I gave it up! In my outspoken way I told God that I was glad to be His child but that this church business was a failure. There was more honest-to-goodness friendliness in the public houses I had lost than in the churches I had found! Never had I met such touchy people, for it just seemed that I had an in-built ability to make hairs stand up on the neck of any respectable church-goer.

Looking back, I see that much of the fault lay at my own door; but I could see that these systems were never going to touch the mass of the people unless there were some radical changes—and change was the last thing anyone seemed to want. 'Leave us alone; ours is the right way' seemed to come from every side.

A well-known evangelist told me that I should give myself to evangelism, that is, the public preaching to the world from tent and hired hall. But yet once again I reacted unfavourably. His world seemed surrounded by microphones and plastic flowers, so to speak, and although I liked him immensely, the idea frightened me. With so much scope for the human personality, I knew I needed much more dealing with by God before He would allow me to take to the stage, if ever.

Where could I find fellowship, open and honest, and uninhibited? Where were the men of disciple calibre that had left their nets to follow the Master?—men and women who lived for Christ and had 'all things common', just as the New Testament showed?—the people who put Communism in the shade? This was my longing, and I wonder if you can understand me?

Now I had forsaken all church buildings and just went along to hear the inspiring messages from the Irish ex-minister. The true Church seemed like a Utopian dream that would never have fulfilment; but I longed for it.

CHAPTER III

DO NOT DISTURB

DAVID, our eldest child, was now about eight years old and attending a private school. It was a good school and he liked it, particularly the Christian headmaster. Quite obviously he was not going to be brilliant, but was showing quite an aptitude for languages already and we knew that, provided we kept him at the right schools, he would get along well and finally hold down a good position in life. At this time I became clearly aware that God was telling me to stop climbing the social ladder. Unless I had heard His voice wrongly, He was telling me to opt out of the rat-race. With public school looming ahead I knew I was going to need to keep on increasing my income to meet the rising costs. So I faced the difficult decision of taking David away from his school and sending him to continue his education at the village school, which was a Church of England school, under the Vicar with whom I had run into so much spiritual trouble. David did not take to the change one little bit and when I heard him repeat what the Vicar had been teaching, I must admit I began to wonder if I had got my leading wrong.

All this time I was making a six-mile journey to the Christian meetings, which were growing more frequent as we found more and more in common. As the responsibilities of the group grew, I realised that I could not shoulder my full load at such a distance and that I would have to move into town. I did not want to have any reservations with God, but found that I had a few that were not so easy to dispense with. For instance, the question of what sort of house I was to live in presented a real problem. The thought of a new semi-detached in a middle-class cul-de-sac sent chills up my spine, but it was obviously where God wanted me to live. I was beginning to learn that the only way really to enjoy my Christian life was to trust and obey God implicitly. My wife was evidently quite happy with this seemingly retrograde step. (Hadn't my blood-mother said she had no ambition and would pull me down!) Now I found her a tower of strength at a time when I was facing what to me was a costly step. It was a beginning of casting behind earthly treasures, which moth and rust consume and which thieves break in and steal.

Father died quite suddenly. He was in his seventies and developed acute pain, stopped eating for a few days and died in the ambulance on the way to hospital. I remember seeing him suddenly jerk his head as we loaded the stretcher and knew he was gone. How good it was to know that in those last few months he had come right back to a personal knowledge of God. The Bible shows us that God rules over everything and that He has not lost control of the world in spite of how grim everything looks to us. I have reason to believe in the sovereignty of God, for I have seen it working so many times. My father's case is just one of them.

A new acquaintance of mine, who must remain anonymous, came to the house one night and I don't expect ever to forget the events as long as I live. This new friend was claiming to have had a revolutionary experience with God, through an encounter with an evangelist on a train. It all seemed real enough, but I was a bit worried that he seemed to 'know it all' so quickly after his conversion. This night I could hear him literally bellowing at my poor old father. He told him that he was a darned old fool for not reading the New Testament —did he not realise that he was near the end of the road and that the judgment for unrepentant sinners was hell? I said to my wife in the adjoining room, 'We can't allow this; I almost feel like going in and knocking his head off'; but the Voice within me was saying, 'Leave it alone.' So I did. From that day on my father began to read the Word of God and blossomed out into a really clear knowledge of Jesus Christ as his own Saviour. Obviously, back in his youth he had been under the sound of the gospel and been quite an active Baptist, I learned. Being constantly with us in the house had whetted his appetite for spiritual things and he had picked up my Bible and looked at Genesis. It was during this time that my friend so audaciously spoke to him and God had used it to jolt my father back to reality. Sad to say, my friend himself did not seem to stand the heat of the way and, just like the parable, grew up very quickly and faded away when things got hot. Actually the last I saw of him was when he borrowed all I had—£30—with a promise of early return and disappeared into the blue. I did not know that the Bible says that you should lend without hope of return. I know now. Perhaps the Lord will one day be able to bring my friend back into the way again.

Father had not long been at rest when I discovered

one of my mother's books on the bookshelf, and opening at the fly-leaf was surprised to read some words she had written when she was a girl, 'I will never leave you or forsake you'—the words of Jesus to His followers. Underneath was her own signature in her maiden name—Rosa Robinson. It was very good of God to let me find that book after all those years.

Dad's funeral service was held at the local crematorium and even there we had a real sense of the presence of God. I remember, too, having to return to the crematorium after the service to take a wreath that had arrived very late. It was a real wintry day, several degrees below freezing as I crossed the forecourt by a short cut, nipping smartly across a sunken concrete area. At least, that's what I thought it was. It turned out to be a frozen pond and I plunged straight through the ice right up to my chest! I drove home shivering and, having removed all my clothes in front of a roaring fire, there was a ring at the bell. My wife appeared in the room and announced innocently, 'It's the insurance man, dear!' It was a day to remember. Now Mum and Dad were gone and my childhood fears of being alone were groundless, for I was married and the father of two bonny children and the question of loneliness never arose.

The job was not going all that well now. On a self-employed basis I relied much upon several large customers I had acquired and a few of these put the cream on the cake. The area I had taken over upon coming South proved to be far less remunerative than I had been given to understand. However, I had built it up from scratch and had employed an assistant when, out of the blue, my two largest accounts went out of business and I found myself down on my knees in prayer. Everything now was a matter for God; there was no area in life in which I did not feel the need for His guidance. I am a natural fighter in the business realm and could have easily started to burn the midnight oil again and pick up with a real effort; but I was convinced that God was speaking to me at the time. It seemed He wanted me to get a steadier position which would leave me more time for His work instead of being under the constant pressure of running a business from my own home. Quite experienced now in dealing with farmers, I was able to find a suitable 'nine to five' position, but at the cost of forfeiting £500 a year in income. By now this did not worry me overmuch, for spiritual things were beginning to dominate my thinking and were becoming the realities to me.

So my ambitious days were behind me. This world which had attracted me for so long was beginning to lose its grip. I had learned by now that the early disciples were baptised into a depth of water, as a token of their burial. They signified by this, I read in the Bible, that they were dead to this present world and lived only for Christ. They had forsaken all to follow Him—they had lost their own lives to gain real life. To take this step became a matter of some urgency with me and soon I was baptised and several fellow-believers laid their hands upon me as I came out of the water. This, I found, was all in the Scriptures and signified that we were all one, for they were associating themselves with me in everything. The Irishman, of whom I had grown so fond, for he was like a spiritual father to me, was the one who plunged me under the water, quoting some words from

Paul's letter to the Philippians to the effect that I would get to know Jesus more by sufferings. Somehow I wanted to do this—to get to know Jesus more and more—and the cost was not the important thing.

It would have been impossible to exaggerate my joy in believing at this time. The people I was mixing with all seemed so real and although I several times had a warning from my inner alarm system, I pushed this voice down when more gracious and learned men offered an explanation. How I wish I had listened more to that still, small voice. How I wish that I had consulted my Bible more personally and not relied so much upon the teachings of others; but at least I have proved that God knows the heart of a man and will bring us through to the truth if we are hungry and will be honest with Him in all things. I would place honesty as the number one prerequisite for a healthy Christian life. 'Some seed fell in good and honest ground and it grew . . . ' We are told that there is none good save God, so this ground in our hearts can only be classified good because it is honest. Things must be brought to the light and faced, whatever the consequences.

What were some of the niggles that I pushed underground? Well, this matter of baptism for instance, like the earlier ceremony around the font, held a few problems. This time not concerning the actual baptism but concerning the rendezvous. We went all the way to a nearby seaside town, a matter of some eighteen miles, to be dipped in a tank of water fitted into the floor of a small hall. There were plenty of churches we could have approached in the city, apart from having a convenient river and everyone having a perfectly useful bathroom in his house. Deep within, I knew that it was having a depth of water to bury me in that really mattered and not the facility of a proper tank. I sensed that we were drawing closer to some Christians than others and that it was important to be dipped in water by the closer associates; whereas the teaching was that we were baptised into one body—that is, one with all Christians. The closer associates, like the friends by the sea where my Irish preacher-friend lived, for instance, were said to be 'standing on clear ground'; that is, were free of drawn-up rules and regulations and were governed locally and did not form part of some larger denominational organisation. I feared that an 'organisation without a name' was arising, but hardly had the strength to seek on after perfection, as I was such a new Christian and had little knowledge.

We all loved to be together and very soon we were meeting every week. Then we met twice a week and finally arranged two meetings on Sundays. On Mondays we gathered for prayer and on Thursdays for a Bible study. On Sunday mornings we invariably broke bread and drank wine together, as the Scriptures said we were to do this often, and in the evening we had a meeting at six-thirty. Don't ask me how it happened; how we congealed into a system so easily, just as everyone predicted we would when we first started to gather so freely. It was a gradual slope rather than a sudden decision to set up something, and no doubt we were genuinely deceived; in fact, probably several of us are deceived to this day, believing we are free just like the religious men that Jesus offered to set free. They could not see it; but they were bound in their tradition and claimed to be in liberty just because they were the sons of Abraham. The blind leading the blind.

I now realise that I was one of the main initiators in the acquiring of special premises to meet in. At one stage I even went so far as to state categoric preference for some heavily lined dark red curtains and royal blue canvas chairs—all nice and ecclesiastical, now that I look back. Obviously it was going to prove more difficult to get the system out of myself than to get myself out of the system! This religiosity was written deep into my mind and obviously needed erasing, even though I had not become a Christian until I was twenty-eight; somewhere along life's way I had imbibed a lot of traditionalism that would have to be dealt with. Come to think of it, I believe someone had the liberty to suggest we bought some floral curtains—they would be more homely; but I wouldn't hear of it! So, before long, we had silver utensils for the bread-and-wine service and we made much of what we termed the 'Lord's Table'.

We had no basis for meetings, no official minister, and so technically we were not bound by rules and regulations. God should have been able to direct us to do whatever He wanted us to do at any given moment. We should have been a flexible container (or wineskin) for the Holy Spirit (or New Wine) to be poured into. You will recall, perhaps, that our Lord Jesus spoke about the folly of putting new wine into old wineskins which are brittle and rigid. The one causes the other to split and there is a loss of wine. Obviously that is how the revivals of the past have petered out because the wineskin has not been suitable to contain the wine.

I had not realised that unwritten liturgy can be as

binding as anything drawn up in Convocation and passed on through the centuries as tradition. For something to be living it has to be a 'this moment' experience and not a mere habit. This does not mean that God may not do some things twice in a row; but it does mean that we must never do something this time just because it was good last time. Deep in the heart of man there seems to be a tendency to form a pattern and do the same thing week after week. Of course, I can see now that it is less costly than a moment-by-moment Christianity. In the formality one can find an opiate for one's conscience and yet still play the part one wants to play. If you are of a retiring disposition, or do not want to become too involved in the cares of others, you can withdraw without being noticed too much. If, on the other hand, you have an outgoing personality, then you can make the best of it and take a prominent part in the organisation. Rarely do we reason the process out in a deliberate way; so often we take the line of least resistance and go along with our natural temperament.

Formality must have the backing of Scripture, of course, and so a convenient text is found upon which to hang the argument. Ours was, 'Let everything be done decently and in order.' How often that text has been used to quench a move of the Holy Spirit I would dread to imagine. Another used frequently is, 'God is not the author of confusion.' Both these are misapplied when used to justify repetition. We quite overlooked the fact that the words concerning order were written to an unruly Corinthian Church. Instead of realising that the apostle was seeking to put right the sin and absolute disorder in their community and in their gatherings together, we applied it to our 'system'. Actually he did not say things should be done in 'an order', but 'in order'—or in an orderly fashion.

It would only be right and helpful to show just how I got on the slippery slope towards formality. The regard for *man* obviously lies deep in the root of this matter.

The man I had first heard preaching continued to visit us twice weekly and, for many years, was the means of our receiving teaching. He was so obviously greatly gifted and such a fine man that I was soon sitting willingly learning at his feet. The only serious reservation I carried for any length of time was his extreme allegiance to a Conference Centre in London and in particular his great deference to one leading man there.

Men are strange creatures; at least I am a strange creature, for there was one incident that made me really uneasy and it all revolved around a cup of tea. It was a conference time; this series of meetings was being held on our home ground, and no one had received a cup of tea before the proceedings began. Everything was thrown into a flurry because the prominent speaker, from the London Conference Centre, had not had a cup of tea. Nor had anyone else, I protested! That was not the point; the great man must be supplied. Now I do not believe that *he* was insisting upon it; but what a fuss was made of the man. I was furious—not much sign of Christian grace showing yet, I'm afraid. This incident so upset my frame of mind that it was quite impossible for me to concentrate when he started to preach.

At this point my eyes alighted on the face of another man. He was elderly and sitting opposite. His eyes and his face told me that he had suffered much pain. In a moment I had forgotten the tea-cups, for there were marks of great grace in that old face. Do you know, I suddenly wanted to be like that old man I had never seen before and gradually, my angry heart began to melt and grow warm within me. Now I started to hear the words coming from the front of that large upstairs room and they were registering deeply on my spirit; the Inner Witness was certainly in tune with this message: 'This child (Jesus) is set for the falling and rising again of many. . . .' They were the words of old Simeon as he lifted the baby Jesus in his arms. He could die peacefully now as he so eloquently expressed: 'Lord, now lettest Thou Thy servant depart in peace, for mine eyes have seen Thy salvation', words that most of us know off 'by head' and not by heart. For the first time they really meant something and I saw that old Simeon was ready for anything. He had seen the Lord. 'This child is set.' It was settled and nothing could alter it. Not even Herod who would try to kill all the children, or the religious crowd who would not have this man to rule over them, could stop Him reaching the end He had come for. It was settled; He was set. Just like old Simeon, I felt ready to die. God had stepped down into His creation in terms of humanity and nothing could stop His purpose from being fulfilled. Not to a palace but to a cattle shed with all its smell and dirt. What a Saviour!

My angry heart had nearly prevented me from hearing this great word of comfort; but an unknown servant had melted me without a word. I had learned that to receive truth demands an attitude of heart, an openness to receive. It is not just a matter of cold doctrine. You can have all that for my part; truth has to be living, in other words to have an effect upon people and do some changing in their lives.

Later I learned that the man who had such a grace-filled face had been an eminent minister and God had called him to come out of institutional Christianity. His wife had not been able to agree with his giving up position and security to follow the Master in such a humble capacity as he had chosen. As she was not in sympathy and often said so publicly, he felt unable to continue preaching. He had also suffered many years of physical pain but served quite happily at the literature table with his heart burning for the Lord. I have heard that Watchman Nee, that great apostle of the Church in the Orient, once referred to this rather unknown man as 'the Womb of the West'. I am sure he wears a crown and I am thankful for what he gave me.

What a day it was, that day of conference; a day when men ministered to me without knowing it. One very handsome young man spent a long time talking to me behind the door. What I could not get over was that during the next week someone told me that this man, Richard, had actually sailed for America two days after talking to me. He had moved there permanently, to live and to minister; but he had been so concerned for my welfare that he had completely failed to tell me of this important move. This really did impress me. If *I* had been going to America, everyone at the conference, if not in the town would have known about it. The marks of godliness were beginning to impress me.

These men had depth about them and I became increasingly taken up by their message. How easy it is to appreciate what is good in men and at the same time accept all their teachings without question, because of their godly character. This was the method that Satan used to enslave me—to convince me that *we* were the Church, that our ground of meeting was *the* true ground. He had been vitally interested from the beginning to tie me down to some group of people, somewhere, with the conviction that they (or we) were 'It'!

These men taught that everything had to be organic and not organised. Having seen that we were 'born' into the family of God by regeneration experience, and that there was nothing official to join, this made sense; a Christian was to continue as he had begun. I could see that if God wanted to take a new direction at any time, then there were no rules to consult, no rails to keep within. The Spirit could shine upon the Word written in the Bible, or use another of His methods of divine guidance, and we only had to follow on. There would be no committees to consult, no votes to be counted, so, all that could stand in the way would be our own natural reactions to the new move—for or against—and if we were prepared for these to be dealt with radically and continually, then God could keep moving us on. It seemed so simple and obvious to me, but I failed to realise the subtlety of the adversary who is said to be a serpent. He deluded me into believing that the absence of something (i.e. rules and regulations) meant freedom. That was merely negative—a teaching about Life. All must be organic; but as I have said, we soon had quite a 'system' on our hands and I could see that only dynamite would shift it.

We had regular meetings, for regular activities; but we had not written anything on paper and had neither membership form nor official leader, and so I reasoned that we were free. We could not possibly be termed a denomination, and thus I argued with many. I can see now that I was deceived.

In spite of a genuine desire to go on into new light and experience we were stuck. Some of us longed for the power and movement of the early church, for we envied their obvious spontaneity. Yet we had tried to settle down around the idea that miracles were for the early days, to *establish* the faith, and that now it was a matter of 'pure faith' without any signs.

We, as a group, were treading familiar ground year by year, occupied with the same truths and coming to a grinding halt. We preached about the executive authority of the church, God's instrument for ruling on earth; but—'Please don't ask us to execute anything! Don't ask us to restore the sick to health or perform any outward sign of our calling.' When I think now of some of the flimsy arguments I put forward, in seeming good faith, against any demonstration of the power of God being seen, I am ashamed.

We preached 'all things in common' and enjoyed a measure of real fellowship together which I could plainly see most other groups did not have; yet when it came to money matters for instance, it was obvious we were pretty tight-fisted. It was going to take more than our meagre entry into the world of 'all things common' to convince outsiders of our deep love for one another. Perhaps some of my closest friends will disagree with what I have said; but for myself, I knew there was a depth of giving that I had not begun to touch and I just could not bring it about in my life, in spite of all the teaching about dying to one's own self-interests and other sound truths being expounded with clarity and fervour. I had the witness that the truths were right, but how to perform them was a different matter altogether; there seemed to be something missing.

We preached spontaneity instead of organisation. But, here again, the local body was not working spontaneously and unless one or two of the prominent members pulled the strings, then the body just did not move; we had puppeteers *making* things happen instead of spiritual elders 'overseeing' what was happening. 'Would you like to give a little message this morning, brother?' (string); 'Perhaps you would care to lead us in prayer?' (another string); and so it went on. Had Paul used a false analogy when he had said, 'The Church, which is His body,' meaning that we were all members one of another, just like arms and legs in a physical body, all taking directions from the One Head? Obviously there was a place for leadership in the Church, but the lack of life in the members caused us alarm.

Things were obviously reaching a desperate stage again with me. In fact, as I look back I realise more and more that it is when I am in this desperate state that God moves, when I am really hungry for something better. After ten years or so together as a group, or local church, I was ready to write failure across everything. Some might ask, 'Why? You have a nice company of people, you get on well together, and it might seem best to leave well alone and settle where you are.'

By this time I read very little else except a magazine that was issued from the Conference Centre in London. My mind had been conditioned to receiving truth in the way that this magazine expressed it and all other literature, to me, fell short of the mark. I suppose there must now be thousands of people in a similar position, Christians whose minds have become closed by constantly reading from one source. The problem is that when one is deceived on a matter like this, one is not in a position to do anything about it. There is not an ounce of criticism in these remarks, for I genuinely believed that all other literature was shallow, dealing with the individual walk of the believer, whereas I had seen that God was doing something corporate in the world. If you had told me, as many did, that I was so corporate-minded that I almost needed a time of fellowship with someone before I would blow my nose, then I would merely have felt sorry for you, that you had not 'seen' the truth that I had been privileged to find. Over this matter, I had hung a large 'Do not disturb' notice on the door of my mind.

How easy it is for us to have fellowship with those who have seen what we have seen, to make truth the ground of friendship instead of our one life in the Lord Jesus Christ. How easy it is for us to make everyone else feel outside the pale and not able to understand our terminology. This only tends to produce innumerable small groups of people, each in possession of some valuable light, praying for all the others to see what they have seen. That is exactly the position of the majority of Churches today. I belonged to one of these groups for years and was totally unaware of it. All I knew was that there was something, somewhere, with a bit more 'go' in it than we had found; but I couldn't see how it could really be, for we had the truth! Any light that I could receive came from the group with which I had fellowship, for, as I have made clear, I read or listened to very little from any other source.

Our young folk were not going to get on very well in our stifling atmosphere; that was painfully obvious, although they seemed a spiritual lot at the time. I feared that they would merely pick up our teaching and cease to be as human as I knew young people ought to be.

What was the answer? Why didn't it work? Where was the power of the Church of God? We were in need of a move forward. 'Do a *new* thing, Lord,' was our earnest cry; 'What ever is needed, then do it.' There was a surprise ahead, for as I cried out sincerely to God, He chose to ignore my 'Do Not Disturb' notice.

CHAPTER IV

DYNAMITE

I DECIDED to accept a position as Sales Manager within the Feed Company. The progression interested me not a bit; it was that I felt it to be the will of the Lord, that it would lead into new paths for Him. One of the main features of this promotion was that it entailed covering a far greater area of the country and coming into contact with many new people and places.

One day, with my senior representative, I was visiting an old-fashioned country miller, in the heart of Sussex. He had recently had a row of new grain silos installed and was very proud of this major step forward. There were several bins, about thirty or forty feet high, and I was determined to show interest in the venture by a personal inspection of the bins from above. So we clambered up the dangerous steps and walked along planks in the roof of the building that housed the bins. In spite of all the constant warnings to 'mind yer 'ead' I walked smack into an iron girder placed conveniently at forehead height.

Two men rushed forward to catch me, for the blow was of such severity that major damage was expected. It would be hard to exaggerate the sound of the collision which reverberated round the empty corn bins, causing much alarm to everyone. Strangely enough, I seemed to suffer no damage at all and soon left the premises, amid strong protestations, insisting that I was perfectly all right.

The next port of call was the local public house for a cheese sandwich and my usual tomato juice. As we sat there I took my glass and neatly poured my drink a few inches to the right of my mouth, straight down my suit. It was obvious that my judgment had suffered. Realising that something was going wrong I left immediately and drove the eighty miles home, before any more symptoms occurred. Apparently things could not have been too bad at the time, for I never hit anything and it had just never dawned on me that I ought not to be driving at all with impaired judgment.

Two mornings later I woke with a terrible headache. It felt as though all the world was sitting on my head. The pressure on the brain made me walk with a stoop and every footfall was like a thunderbolt. The doctor diagnosed delayed concussion and ordered a complete rest and a darkened room for several weeks. No reading or writing; just rest. Now that's a thing I don't go much on by nature. I don't like to be sitting still; but it was here that God was to meet with me in a new way.

My business house wrote during the illness for me to consider a further step of promotion—a much more senior position of management within the London office of the company. Clearly I knew it was not to be. As I prayed quietly and waited before the Lord I was able finally to close the door on the offer of a short-list. By declining this important step I knew that I was sealing myself from future advancement, but it had to be done.

Some friends offered me a room in their quiet house by the sea. It would mean a week away from the family which was really a necessity, for by this time we had two very noisy additions—boys within a year of each other—

and they could not understand that 'Daddy must be quiet.' The family now consisted of David aged sixteen, Josslyn twelve, Jason two and Matthew one.

Away in the quiet house of my friends I did not obey doctor's orders. After two days the pressure on my head began to lift a little and so, whenever my friends were out of the room, (and I spent most of the day alone), I took John Wesley's *Journal* from the bookshelves. It absolutely gripped me. The singlemindedness of the man made a deep impression upon me and I saw in a flash that I had been paddling in very shallow water as a Christian. This man had been a one-hundred-per-center and I rather wished I had read about him earlier when the Methodists had tried to point me to his works. Nevertheless, I really knew that this was God's time for me to be reading the book, for every page lived to me.

When I returned home I was on fire for God and shared everything with the friends with whom I was meeting. They greeted me with the news that they felt I had to take things easy, that I had been far too active; whereas I told them that I had been slothful and my Christian life had been lived at half-cock. Looking back, I can see that there was something of the truth in both, although I could not see that at the time.

My walk with God was beginning to be of a much more personal nature. It was not that I felt any less committed to my brethren but that somehow I was hearing the voice of God much more clearly on specific issues. Until this time every decision in life had been a matter of fellowship and sometimes the discussion could take hours over a most simple issue.

For instance, I clearly heard the Lord speaking to my

spirit concerning a move into a certain smaller house down in the centre of town. It was an old terraced house right on the main roundabout. It was a terribly noisy spot for traffic and the main line trains seemed almost to run through the bedroom. There was virtually no garden for the children and other amenities were noticeably missing, yet I knew it was God's will. During a time of prayer a 'sister' had quoted a message from the Bible concerning the old prophet Ezekiel. 'I sat where they sat' was the message and I knew that the Holy Spirit had applied that to me quite personally at the time. ('They' were the people living in the crowded centre of town.) As I drove home from the meeting I heard the clear, yet inaudible voice of God say, 'There is the place for you,' and there was no mistaking the word.

It was a major departure for me to declare to the friends that I did not want their views on the intended move; if they had a specific word from God, then I would welcome it, otherwise I could do without all the natural good advice upon which we had relied for so many years. Just one person spoke to me; he was one of the elders in whom we had recognised a pastoral gift and acknowledged it although there was nothing official in the recognition. He said he felt sure that the move was right and that he had prayed much about it. As I moved from one home to another, by faith, the Lord honoured the step. The long-awaited purchaser of my old property made a firm offer at the very moment that the removal van was at the new house, and the estate agent had to come to the new address to find me.

My business associates thought I was mad leaving a large new house in a respectable area and moving right into the dingy centre of town. On top of this I had refused obvious promotion. There were far greater surprises in store but neither they nor I had any idea of what the Lord was leading up to in His own way. I had peace and that was all that mattered. The Bible teaches that we should 'let the peace of God rule (or umpire) in our hearts', and I knew the umpire had not declared me 'out' on this move. It was all very simple as long as I did not get my natural mind working overtime trying to understand what God was doing. He had promised in His Word to lead me a step at a time and I was just beginning to learn the elementary steps of a life of faith. My responsibility was to trust and obey and He would take full responsibility for the outcome, and His plan would unfold in His time.

It was about this time that the first rumblings of dynamite were heard. One night, sitting with my wife, I closed the day in prayer. Suddenly I found myself involved in an 'experience' for I seemed to be soaring upwards and words of praise were just pouring out of my mouth. At the time we had just entered into a much fuller dimension in our married life together and, after seventeen years, this seemed so wonderful, that I just expressed my deep appreciation to our heavenly Father for bringing this about. Through the years I had not been really faithful as a husband, in spite of wanting to be; but my wife had never forsaken me. This night the prayer was simply marvellous and quite exhilarating. When I came down again I was somewhat alarmed. 'Was that all right, dear?' I asked. My wife hastily assured me that the prayer was quite wonderful and that she had never heard me pray in such a manner before.

Before many days were passed I had attributed this experience to the devil. For years my mind had been well and truly conditioned against experiences, particularly ones that you could not understand! I reasoned that I must have somehow got myself into a state of passivity and been 'taken over' by some other force. It was all very dangerous, I concluded, and so I fought well shy of the supernatural that had presented itself to me so unexpectedly.

God was answering my heart cry for a new thing, but I did not know it. Even the concussion was, in His economy, perhaps the only way to get me to be still for a while and to wait upon Him. From literature that I would not normally have had any time for, God had taken the opportunity to show me something new.

. . . . .

The same brother who approved my house move went on holiday with his family to South Wales and passed through the South Cotswolds *en route*. They decided to call in on some friends who had trodden a similar pathway to us in days gone by; that is, had sought to know what it meant to live as a fellowship and believed that God's thought for this end of the age was a corporate thought—a Church that had all things common. Like us, they had willingly subscribed to the teaching that in all things the Lord Jesus Christ should have pre-eminence. The visitors were amazed to find that these friends had 'gone Pentecostal', or were now believing in an experience which they called the Baptism in the Holy Spirit, saying that all sorts of gifts would follow from such an experience. In short, the lack of New Testament power was due to the lack of a New Testament experience. From what I can gather, they stayed up pretty late discussing it all before moving on towards their holiday resort.

The first morning that the family spent in Wales the husband found himself almost unable to move. Something quite serious had happened to his back, and it was evident that the assistance of a doctor was needed. The pronouncement was soon made that he needed absolute rest (another one brought to a standstill) and that the holiday would have to be abandoned. They decided to call me in to assist with the return journey, when their daughters pressed Mum and Dad to seek the God who does miracles. As they again turned in prayer to the Lord and persisted, they felt directed to seek the assistance of a nearby chemist. He said he knew a minister who might help and finally found his address, which was some miles away. In spite of great pain they managed to get to this man who quickly laid him on a table and placed his hands on his back, gave some manipulation, and pronounced him perfectly fit to enjoy his holiday. A new man ran out of the house to the jubilation of his family who saw their holiday was restored by the intervention of a prayer-answering God.

The next thing we received back at base was a postcard from South Wales to the effect that God was showing them a new way.

By now, we were gathering every morning of the week at six-thirty for prayer and God was meeting us. How well I remember hoping that the new thing they were seeing would confirm the new fervour we were experiencing! It proved to be the very thing we were in need of.

. . . . .

Soon my business activities were resumed, although I was still somewhat curtailed by pressure on top of my head. One night, on my extended travels, I found myself in the same Cotswold village where we first met up with the new Pentecostal move. One of the friends had a hotel and I was asked to speak to their group, which I did, for the best part of an hour. Towards the close I felt that I should share with them the need we had for much more liberty and spontaneity, both in worship and in the power realm. I told them of my own experience in prayer with my wife, of the sense of being borne up on wings and of my subsequent denial of it all. I clearly expounded to them how necessary it was to keep two feet solidly on the ground and not to be blown about all over the place with experiences.

Have you ever seen a revolving stage, the sort of thing they have in a cabaret show where one dance band will disappear while the other one is swinging into position? One plays its way out and the other one simultaneously plays its way in. That is just what I felt begin to happen to me. One moment I was facing the circle of maybe fifteen friends and I held the stage. Now they had the initiative and on centre stage was a young girl of about twenty years. 'Don't you think you're in danger of closing your mind to the very thing that you're asking God to do?' she asked. My back was to the wall and, suddenly, I was aware that I was fighting very hard to maintain my ground, and having to use all I knew both from the Scriptures and from my personal experience. I had always reckoned that assertive argument was a sign that I might be wrong. After all, if I were right, what was I getting so worked up about? Nevertheless, on this occasion, I continued to fight very hard.

From this time on my contact with the Cotswold folk increased. I had no intention of returning this way when I left for the South and the running tracks; but here I was calling in at the small hotel whenever the opportunity afforded itself. They had sent me on books about this power for the Body of Christ; but I was not really impressed. There was virtually no mention of the corporate way of living and so I tended to write it all off as shallow, although I noticed that a few of the younger believers seemed to find something attractive in the literature.

I was in a spot. Would anyone even understand how I felt? Some folk said I needed to get baptised in the Holy Ghost and start speaking in other tongues as they did at Pentecost when the Holy Spirit was poured out on the waiting believers in Jerusalem. They pointed out that there was no power for the Christian unless he knew this experience. I had known precious little miracle-working in my life, I had to admit, but I knew somehow there was power within me. Others said it was perfectly obvious that I had been baptised in the Spirit and that I ought just to acknowledge the teaching and bring others into it thereby. Most of my associates said there was no such experience anyway, as you automatically received the Holy Spirit at conversion. They were quite adamant that there was not such a thing as a second blessing.

Everyone used Scripture to prove his point and I became just plain confused. Was there something more? If there was, then I really wanted it, yet I had to be sure that what I received was from God and not something from Satan to trip me and those in the flock over which

I shared oversight. The whole Church in England was in such need of release, and I wanted so much to be of some use to the Lord towards setting people free from religion into vital Christianity.

We had received teaching over the years to the effect that the gifts of the Spirit were only for babies, that they ceased once the early Church was established, and that today it was mainly counterfeit work that was being seen. To my shame, I recollect that I never personally investigated the Scriptures, but took all that came from men more learned in the Word of God.

One night I was motoring to a rectory tucked away in the Oxfordshire countryside to hear a man preach that I knew would emphasise the need for enduement with power. (Strange how even seeking after something of the Holy Spirit drew me into contact with other Christians again, for I certainly would not have crossed a rectory threshold for spiritual food a few months previously!) As I drove in pouring rain along that unknown dark road I reasoned things out with myself: I'm sure I have received the Spirit, for it says plainly in the book of Acts that if you repented (which I had done) and were baptised (which I had been), then as a result there was a double outcome to be enjoyed. First, you had all your sins remitted. Well, I was quite sure about that. There was no sense of guilt at all; I had been cleared by a merciful God. Secondly, it said you would receive the gift of the Holy Spirit.

Perhaps, with me, it was not so much the Holy Spirit Himself that I had a prejudice against but the manifestations that had accompanied the first outpouring. Perhaps I did not want to speak in other languages or to speak supernaturally inspired messages of prophecy as the early Christians did. I remember hearing the gifts years ago in what was called a Bible Pattern Church and I was not impressed; particularly by the ladies and their prominent use of the gift of tongues which rather frightened me at the time. Since then, in the Cotswold hotel, I had heard a beautiful tongue and a very helpful interpretation. Would God give bad gifts to His children? It was unthinkable!

I determined there and then that I had received the Holy Spirit according to God's promise and that I could also speak in tongues. So, I opened my mouth, moved my lips and my tongue and deliberately made a noise. I did not listen closely to what it sounded like, but was soon aware that I was speaking quite fluently in another language. As long as I kept my natural mind from trying to interfere with the gift it just flowed on. So I kept my mind on the dark wet road and spoke in tongues all the way to the rectory, which was some twenty minutes away. Now I felt very pleased with myself, which was not a very godly sort of attitude, but I suppose I was relieved that the months of striving and argument were over.

Once or twice afterwards I had second thoughts about it all because of the lack of spontaneity in the manner of receiving; but I realised that my life was definitely on a new plane. Praising God was much more real and I knew things were going to be different. Just how different I had no idea!

. . . . .

On returning home I was struck by the heavy atmosphere that often characterised our prayer meetings and which was in such contrast to the rejoicing within my own heart. How vividly I recall one particular Saturday morning when we started with a long, long silence. It was not one of those holy silences where, in the stillness, one is aware of the presence of God; but one of those awfully embarrassing times when you know that everyone is at a dead-end and unable to put any heart-felt words together. Suddenly God spoke to me by the Holy Spirit, or Inner Witness. He said, 'You have no need to lack prayer or praise at any time, for you can use the gift I have given you publicly—you can speak in an unknown tongue!'

Now I was really on the spot. Thoughts began to pour through my mind: 'The elders aren't here and I've not discussed it with them'; 'I'll be up before the Sanhedrin for this'; and so on. Then a reprieve presented itself to me. There was no one there to interpret and the Bible clearly states that there must be one there to interpret if this gift is used in public. Back came the word of the Lord to my inner man, 'They'll never know they can interpret unless someone speaks in an unknown language.' The logic was undeniable: how could they know if they had a supernatural gift unless there was an opportunity for its use? The one gift so obviously depended upon the other in this case.

With perspiration literally running down my legs I spoke out in a tongue and I listened carefully to every syllable on this occasion—it sounded awful. Suddenly the room was full of activity. Everyone wanted to pray; probably they were overcome with embarrassment as they had never heard anything like it before. The whole company had been behind us when we went to hear more about these gifts at a conference in the Oxfordshire hotel; but to be confronted with their use unannounced was an obvious surprise. After the spate of praying there was a long pause during which I died several deaths. There was not going to be an interpretation, I feared. Now what would the elders say? Tongues without interpretation would undoubtedly bring the accusation of Corinthian confusion.

A young girl convert started to speak out a message of praise and I realised it was from the book of Psalms, but she was not reading her Bible. Afterwards she said that as I was speaking in the unknown language, these words had just come to her, that she had not thought them up. She was so young in the faith, but I remember she was one who had appreciated the books which had been sent to try to get me into the current move of the Holy Spirit that was touching so many in our land. It was all so obviously from God that we were excited and some came home to breakfast with me to talk it over.

'I knew straight away that it was from God,' said one young man. 'Oh, how was that?' I enquired. 'Well, there was so much more love in your voice than usual!' I thanked him for the back-handed compliment.

Some were delighted that there was a new move afoot, but others felt it was dangerous and the issue caused division, for it was apparent that some did not want much alteration from the way in which we had been going. There was such an obvious problem arising that we agreed to drop the pursuance of the gifts in public, at least for a while. To me this still registers as a period during which the Holy Spirit was grieved and when the enemy made inroads; but it was done for the sake of others and, as best we could, we kept the lid on things. The motto was 'Business as usual'. However, the Holy Spirit was moving and very soon the dynamite we had longed for was beginning to explode.

The night of the big bang was not far away. It was a Monday evening time of prayer when things seemed to ignite at several places in the room at the same time. Some who were pent up in themselves found release. One believer stood up and made an unprompted confession of having constantly deceived us over a certain matter. Meanwhile one young lady began to make loud groanings and slipped to the floor as though being delivered from some strong power of evil. All this was the signal for one man to get up and leave, but after one pace forward, he hit the floor face first as though he had been pole-axed. I must confess that I thought he was dead. He was a violent man, having suffered terribly during the War and had previously felled others when under provocation because the powers of evil were driving him. Now he lay as slain at our feet. When we had prayed for him he recovered and as a result decided to seek permanent employment. The room was a hive of activity and I was so glad that those who were constantly pleading for decency and order were absent.

Evidently we had the beginnings of a revival on our hands, for Satan's entrenchment in many lives had been dramatically exposed. Furthermore, we 'mature' elders were made aware of our inexperience and lack of discernment, having appeared to be competent during all the peaceful years of predictable routine. At this stage we were unable to take full advantage of this divine visitation.

As the time went on other gifts began to appear, and a whole new realm of the supernatural was opening up to us, the realm of the invisible, which the Bible teaches is the real realm, 'for the things which are seen are transient, but the things which are unseen are eternal'. It was a realm which we had spoken about; but we had never been able to get into the reality of it all.

The first gift of prophecy came in a remarkable way. We had received no teaching about it at all; but in a moment of need the Lord just simply and beautifully gave the gift. During a time of prayer for a specific situation one leading member of the group suggested a halt to wait upon God, so that He might inspire vital prayer and take away the formality. After a few moments of silence a very authoritative voice spoke out: 'Thus saith the Lord, I will bless you . . . ' A distinct and encouraging prophecy followed from God, when the operator of the gift knew nothing of the mode of operation at all. The effect of this prophecy was to 'lift' the meeting and send it forward purposefully.

Soon, just as it says in the book of the Acts concerning the last days, we found that dreams and visions were coming to both old and young. These held obvious messages and provided a source of new help to people in bondage and it was evident that some had a God-given ability to interpret these visions and dreams, just as others could interpret a tongue in another language. Furthermore, we were beginning to be able to distinguish between what was genuinely coming from God and what was merely the product of the dreamer's unconscious mind.

My eldest son, David, had been a lifelong sufferer from

asthma and hay-fever. As a child the asthma was serious, but over the years we had all come to accept the limitations and discomfitures involved. David had to miss the strenuous sports at school, which was a disappointment to him. He could go nowhere near dust or feathers. It was impossible for him to wash with soap, or to tolerate any flowers in the house at any time. He had learned to live with a constant nose-twitching and body irritation.

One week-end he went to a young peoples' house-party in West Kent and, during the time there, the preacher took an unusual step. He announced that he knew that there were certain ailments in the room and that he would willingly pray for the sufferers if they would acknowledge their need. One of these 'words of knowledge' concerned a young man suffering from asthma. David states that, although he acknowledged that the information was right, he did not feel happy about the presentation and, for some reason, held back. When he related all this to me I was quick to challenge him that really he did not believe he could be healed. 'But I do!' he protested. 'Oh yes, you believe God *can* heal you, but you don't believe He wants to do it *now*,' I said. He immediately asserted that he was quite certain that the Lord could do the healing at that very moment. Now I was in a spot—I was on that revolving stage again—for he was obviously in fulness of faith and I was being exposed myself.

In an instant I found myself saying, 'Kneel down here and I'll pray for you. When I touch your nose you are to release all the faith you have and, as we agree together, God will heal you.' I simply thanked God for the healing in the name of Jesus Christ and touched his nose. As I made the contact it seemed that his nose was the size of a pumpkin to me, and instantly I heard him saying, 'Praise the Lord.' That was quite an unusual expression for David at the stage he was at then, being a quiet, introvertive lad. 'What's happened?' I asked. 'Every vestige of irritation left my body at the moment you touched me,' he replied. I instructed him to go downstairs and to stuff soap in his nose and come upstairs again to show me. This he did immediately and has not wheezed or itched since that moment.

There was a brief contesting when he had a slight cold after a few days, but we held out in faith and he has not had any trouble at all for two whole years. Now he has a feather pillow and is active in sports and is in no way inhibited.

A new realm of authority in Christ was being discovered and I was just thrilled. At the same time I was mystified by those who were so cautious of everything. For myself I could not wait at all, and began to run before I could walk. Impatient to grow up in spiritual power, I had 'laid hands' on several people before long, for everyone came for help now and it seemed pointless to turn any way. Some were quite wonderfully helped, others were not. Again I was brought to a puzzling position. Was this realm, too, going to hold problems? Was there nothing that was plain and straightforward? It was obvious, quite soon, that I was a mere babe in this realm and that I was going to need to keep very near to God, to hear His voice clearly if I were not going to make endless mistakes. My son had living faith and was not just experimenting with healing to see if it worked! He said it was evident to him from the Bible that Jesus came to make people whole and that the physical as well as the spiritual (if you can separate them) was obviously prominent in His dealings with men.

Now one looks back on a few years of new joy, new depths of experience, new power and much new light from the Word of God. There have been many failures, but these have only driven me back to God for the answer—sometimes in near despair, I admit; but they have been profitable. The increase of fellowship with so many Christians outside our rather exclusive circle of believers has also been a startling symptom of the coming of the Holy Spirit into my life in this more positive way.

CHAPTER V

A BID FOR FREEDOM

'I HAVE learned, in whatsoever state I am, therein to be content!' This I knew to be freedom indeed and well I remember the derision of my work-fellows as I stated this to be my aim for living, that no circumstances should affect me. As you can imagine, I was told that this was impossible idealism.

At the time of writing, it seems that the whole of the youth of the world is rising up after freedom. There is no obvious organisation and yet it is impossible not to be impressed by the universal nature of the uprising. The restrictions that would have been accepted a few years ago as part and parcel of living on earth are now being wholeheartedly rejected. Man is unsatisfied and strives against the establishment.

I cannot for one moment condone the bitterness and violence in youth, but I do understand the desire for something better than what the churches and governments of our generation have offered them. I can understand their failure to accept a society that offers so little. Of course they must reject a middle-class morality that has oodles of false standards; that judges a man by the length of his side-burns and that for years could accept a girl in a bathing costume but not in a skirt that was above her knee; a society that is steeped in class distinction and racial discrimination; a society that defends peace by going to war. They have seen through the propaganda of every party that offers happiness in return for more goods, that is tied to a higher-standard-of-living god. They are hopelessly confused and openly state that they are in revolt but often do not understand why. Things are wrong, that is all.

There is only one basic problem, that Jesus Christ is not yet in His right place. Real freedom is only found in becoming his willing servant. He is the only Leader who measures up to His message. He not only preaches at you, He comes down and lives in you and sets you free from tyrant self. We are our own worst enemy, in a sense. Do you remember, right at the beginning of this little book, how I made the discovery that I was the trouble, not the other fellow? Well, let me now tell you some of the practical ways in which Jesus Christ has set me free since I came to know Him personally and let Him take over the government of my life.

Let us start with sex, a problem to anyone who really wants a clean conscience, and free-love is no answer to that! For most of my life I have been plagued with a sex problem, and since I had become a Christian I knew I did not have to live in a condemned state of mind, because Jesus took my punishment on the Cross at Calvary—but deep down inside me I not only wanted to be forgiven, I wanted to be free from the nagging scourge itself.

Even though I was married and loved my wife very dearly it was impossible for me to overcome this great attraction for the opposite sex. It made no difference to me where I was; a prayer meeting was no different from a business cocktail party. If one of the opposite sex was sitting in any sort of exposed position, then the place became hell on earth to me. (If you are free of this dreadful soul-destroying power, then do not criticise but be deeply grateful.) For me, it was a full-time occupation to keep my eyes in the right place and I could concentrate on little else at the same time. Driving a car was a nightmare, for my head would turn at every attractive girl that passed. Will-power was useless. Many a time I have pulled up in a lay-by and wept as I cried to God, 'Oh, take this away, please.'

Sometimes, after a day of defeat, I hardly knew how to go home; I was so ashamed. I knew there had to be a release somewhere or the whole of my Christianity was in jeopardy, for the Bible teaches that if you resist the devil 'he will flee'. Well, frankly, when I resisted him on this issue, he did not flee and I reasoned that if the Bible were wrong on this, then it could be wrong in other matters too and the whole of my eternal salvation was on shaky ground. Yet, I knew I was one of God's children and had a wonderful peace at having been born into His royal family. I was a King's son and I knew it; but oh! I did so want to live a life that was clean and worthy of Him. All this awful lust was not fitting for someone who could say with such assurance, 'God is my Father.'

Do you know, God heard those cries from the depths of my being and met me in a most wonderful way? However, once again, I put up the most tremendous resistance against the truth that always sets us free when allowed to have its full sway. I did it in ignorance and He had mercy upon me. It all happened like this:

One day I was again in business in the Cotswolds area and took the opportunity to call on my friends in the evening. One, you may remember, owned a hotel, and the other had an outfitter's shop in the High Street. The daughter of the shopkeeper had just returned from Holland and related to us an experience concerning men for whom I had the greatest respect, for I had heard of their faith and of the dangers that they had faced in the service of Jesus Christ. This young lady said they had prayed for her and she had been delivered from the power of an evil spirit. She testified to the release that she had found in her life from that moment, but did not go into details.

My back went up, I can tell you. Evil spirits indeed! Where did they think we were, in the heart of Africa dealing with witch-doctors?

The conversation developed and finally the family with the 'delivered daughter' left, while I was still waxing eloquent against the idea of evil spirits having anything to do with Christians. As the night drew on I realised I was getting up in the corner again, for it was gradually dawning on me that this strong sexual urge of mine was not coming from a temptation outside me, which I could resist; rather it was firmly rooted in me. I had no time or opportunity to resist, for the thing had control of me before I had a chance to start.

Now, if this really was a sort of spirit-personality within me, then I needed help, for I knew that I could not cast it out myself; it was a job for the Lord. If there was something down inside me that was not convertible, then it had better be got out—the issues were clarifying. Right up to that time I had either been fighting the sin with all I had, or else trying to leave it for God to do, according to my doctrinal view at the time, or my degree of despair. All I knew was, that up until then nothing had worked.

There was just the hotelier and his wife with me when I, fully and frankly, said I felt I had a personal problem along this line. Ten years a happy Christian; but with this colossal skeleton in my cupboard that just threatened to ruin everything! 'If you had to put a name to this thing, what would you call it?' they asked. 'Well, I suppose I would call it a spirit of lust,' I replied. 'Of course,' added my hostess; 'and when were you last plagued with it?' I confessed that I had been troubled with it while driving to their hotel, and also that I had been wrestling with the thing all evening; in fact, I never had a free moment! She suggested that it should be dealt with there and then; that we had authority over evil spirits according to the Word of God and that she was sure that if her husband were to pray for me, then I would be delivered. She went on to tell me how she had been set free from a dominating spirit of fear, through the ministry of Edgar Trout, who pioneered with such authority against the powers of evil.

Right up to that evening I had hardly countenanced the presence of evil spirits in England, let alone in myself! Yet, now, deep down within my heart, I knew we had arrived at the truth. It probably went right back to my blood-mother and her influence over me. It seemed quite clear to me that this foul spirit had found a habitation in my body to express all his vile desires and I had no doubt that I had given adequate grounds for his entry in my early life. All the talk about principalities and powers had come much nearer home now. I had always had them in 'heavenly places', which is quite right; but where is heaven? It is much nearer than we think, for Jesus Himself said: 'The kingdom of heaven is within you.' Some of these powers, of which the heavens were to be cleared, needed to be cleared out of me!

Willingly I knelt down in that very small lounge and I noticed that the clock said just on midnight. Eddie began to pray softly but firmly, and I willed this foul thing away from me in co-operation, as best I knew how. All I knew was I wanted to be pure and to get rid of this unclean influence in my life for ever.

From right down in the pit of my stomach something began to rise. It felt like a dark green slimy substance and it came right up through my chest, as it were, and straight out of my head. Then it was as though someone came along with a sack of pure white flour and poured it down into my body. I felt clean and I knew I had been delivered. My friends did not look so sure, strangely enough; but I knew, and the weeks and months only proved the matter.

How wonderful to be free from that daily torment of mind, to be able to meet men and women as equals and not to feel so inferior to women. Free, too, from that fear that they knew what was going on in my mind towards them. How great to be able to drive without the continual battle with my eyes. My wife shared in the joy of my release, for she knew my desire to be faithful and had witnessed my sorrow in the past.

Now I was beginning to understand that Jesus really wanted me to enjoy the utter freedom that He had died to purchase for me on the Cross of Calvary. Not just freedom from guilt, because He had died for our forgiveness; but freedom from the power of evil in daily living.

Holiness became a practical possibility now and the desire to be perfect in every thought and deed of life became a deep thirst. You see, I had been freed from the one great sin that dominated me and I knew now that anything was possible.

I realised that things were beginning to happen now; it was not a case of learning a lot of objective truth and hoping it would somehow produce a holy life. Truth had become powerful. 'You will know the truth and the truth shall make you free.' The Holy Spirit, since I had much more specifically accepted Him, was now beginning to lead me into 'all truth', as it says in the Bible. Jesus said, 'I am the truth' ('reality' is another translation), and I was beginning to discover that only He is true and real; everything else was false and fading, that Jesus was the only Absolute Reality. Way back I remember struggling with something written by Bertrand Russell to the effect that man needed a New Absolute, that everything needed somehow to be new. Well, I realised that I had found that absolute in the person of Jesus Christ, and that I had actually received His new life. Oh, I knew I had a long way to go, much more to learn, only now it all seemed so gloriously attainable.

Maybe I have not made myself very clear. It was just that if God had delivered me from my dirty thoughts and looks and actions that had plagued me all my life, then I knew He could do anything. He was not just Almighty 'up there', but that right here in our world He could do anything. He could deliver anyone who really wanted to be free and came to him in honesty. I began to desire that the Lord would give me the ability to help others as I had been helped.

Since that time much water has flowed under the bridge and we have learned that Satan's filth is on the increase and that members of the church are by no means immune from it all. God is doing a cleansing work right now and purifying His own people. Deception is on every hand as spiritualism, black magic and satanism grow rapidly in our land. Having failed to find satisfaction in material things, many are turning to the mystic, pressing into realms of fortune-telling and occult practices such as glass-moving and levitation, which the Bible says should be left alone, and they are being contaminated by evil spirits. The Lord has promised that when the enemy comes in like a flood, as is happening, He will raise up a standard against him. He is doing this now, I am sure; men with clear authority over demons are coming forth across the whole world.

Freedom from sexual sin: one more stepping-stone on the way to knowing that fulness of freedom 'in whatsoever state I am'. That is the goal: complete satisfaction, at all times, in Christ. By now I ought to have learned, that if one seeks to move on, then one never knows what God is going to touch next, and so it proved to be in a very short time.

. . . . .

I was driving home from Hampshire, through Sussex. It was as I was coming along the lovely A272, one of my favourite roads, that the Lord took me by surprise. It was in the cool of the evening and I had been busy all day. My mind was not consciously thinking about God or spiritual things, when suddenly my car became filled with gentle light. In all my experience I had never known such a phenomenon, and no doubt the sceptic would have many quite natural explanations; but I never had any such thoughts, for I knew it was the Lord and His presence quietly convinced me in a moment that He had a special job for me to do. There was no audible voice, but just a deep sense that I had been called. I gripped the wheel resolutely and drove home.

Here was another shock to our old way of thinking. I had always nursed the idea that there was something quite wrong for a man to be a full-time Christian worker. All the dangers of his losing touch with the man in a secular job had presented themselves to me, and I was convinced that the Church was suffering from professionalism above everything else. It had become two classes, the preachers and the workers, and thus lost its usefulness in the world. Therefore, I had purposed never to join the ranks of those outside regular secular employment.

The conviction steadily grew, however, that God had spoken and so I shared it with others in authority back within the group. There was certainly no real sign of encouragement forthcoming, although to me the call was clear. I decided that I would just wait until they mentioned it to me again; but meanwhile sought counsel from a spiritually mature man of God who lived in Richmond, for I knew he had a real call of God. He pointed out that when Paul and Barnabus were separated to the work by the Holy Spirit the elders were fasting and praying; so providing we were employing these spiritual methods there was no problem; but this fact he doubted. I knew he was right and decided to mention it once more to my fellow-elders. This time there was complete agreement, that my gift was more than local, and that we should look to the Lord to show His timing.

All the implications now became clear to me as I was gently pressed by God into a serious consideration as to when I should discontinue my secular employment. There had been no offer of financial support from the body of Christians with whom I met and, for a man with four children, it was no mean thing to consider. I knew I was going to have to live entirely by faith, that is, I was going to have to trust God to provide somehow for my family, to pay the mortgage, the food, the clothes, the heating and everything else that makes such a demand upon us in these days of high cost of living. My being totally unknown as a minister and being entirely unsponsored by any Christian organisation made it a very real decision for me to face. Perhaps you are thinking that my faith was not very strong.

Like Gideon, in the Old Testament, the call was a bit much for me to face up to and so I asked God for a sign that He really was with me, that there really would be fruit from the ministry and that He would not allow me to make a foolish mistake. Gideon put a fleece upon his threshing floor and said that if, in the morning, it were wet, while all the ground around was dry, then he would know that God was with him. I had been very exercised that any work God gave me to do should be original and that I should not build upon another man's foundation. This I knew meant to me that I would be working with raw material, people who were not ready made by another's ministry. Don't ask me why I was thus exercised, for I don't know. It must have been God-inspired, I should think, because I had no real love for the non-Christian; in fact, I was pretty well cold towards unbelievers. It had been a very long time since I had been instrumental in bringing anyone to conversion, although I had been on fire in this direction in my early Christian days. The modern methods and machinery of evangelism had put me off and I had even found that evangelical Christians, on the whole, were rather stiff and holier-than-thou in attitude. To me, I knew there was a more potent and effective way of presenting the Gospel than anything I had witnessed in my lifetime and this ideal was all I could accept as the normal. It all sounds rather critical, I'm afraid.

So for the first time in my life I put out a fleece. 'Lord, someone must be clearly converted, right out of the world, *this day*, or I'll know You're not with me.' Within a few hours I had panicked and, for fear that I had been too dogmatic, asked the Lord to extend it to a week; but He had heard the first time.

That very evening I was looking out of the premises where the believers gathered; it was an upstairs room and through the window I saw the back of a man. 'There he goes; that's your man.' It was the voice of the Spirit speaking. I was quite taken by surprise but found myself running down the stairs and up the road after this lone figure. He was familiar to me by sight, for I had seen him in the town before and felt sympathy for him in his plight. He was obviously suffering from a severe heart condition and could only walk very slowly. His age was about thirty-five, I guessed.

As I stopped him and looked into his blue face, I told him that God had sent me to tell him that He wanted him to trust His Son Jesus Christ. There was nothing that Jesus could not do for him, I said, fumbling in my inside pocket for some literature to hold his attention. I soon realised that the small gospel tract I held out showed a medicine bottle on the front, and that this man urgently needed physical healing. However, he had other thoughts uppermost in his mind. 'Can He give me a bed tonight?' he bluntly asked. 'Yes,' I replied. 'You can sleep in my house if you wish.' He told me that he had slept rough in an empty house the night before.

He agreed to come and sit in our meeting until it was time to come home with me. There was only a handful of us and during the evening, quite informally, we felt it would be good to remember the Lord by breaking bread and drinking some wine together. It was very seldom that we did this during the week, but now it seemed right, so one of us went to borrow some bread while another poured the wine. Dennis, the man from the street, weighed up the gospel message which had been simply presented to him. For what seemed an age, he hesitated before taking the bread; but finally stretched forth his hand and took Jesus Christ as the Bread of life. There and then he entered into the kingdom of heaven and has been following the Master ever since.

Suddenly, I realised my fleece had been answered. God was in earnest over this huge step of my giving up secular employment. Twice more, I am afraid, I put God to the test because the step was so important and each time He answered immediately with a confirmation, and so I gave three months' notice and, like Abraham, went out 'not knowing whither he went'. My business house thought I had taken final leave of my senses; but I had peace in my heart and knew that all was well.

What has it been like since we took this step? Before we took for granted our regular income (knocking on

£2,000 a year). Now we often have the pleasure of seeing our needs met at the eleventh hour by people who could not have known our immediate situation. We have learned how weak our faith is and how to cry unto the Lord in reality without phrasing pretty prayers. We felt clearly that, for us, God had said we were not to publish our needs or to send out prayer-letters, which can so easily be a form of solicitation. He would supply our needs if we would look to Him alone. Alas, we have sometimes failed, by letting go the slight hint when up against it, and have needed to repent of such disgraceful methods when we have the Bank of Heaven at our disposal.

There have been disappointments since coming out into the work of the Lord, and I suppose they fall under two headings. The first is clearly that, although our ministry has been blessed, there has been nothing like the power that I saw once when I put my final fleece before the Lord. There I asked for a manifestation of His power without any effort of my own—and He did it. The power of the Holy Spirit just fell on the meeting and no one could move or speak afterwards. I took this as the 'norm' from then on and confidently expected it to happen wherever the Lord sent me. Looking back now I know that I half expected to start with meetings on an Albert Hall scale and move on from there!

Instead of what I expected, God has been taking me into a much deeper relationship with Himself and dealing with me until I am no longer such a mixture—sometimes giving Him the glory and sometimes taking it for myself—until I can help people from a pure motive and not just 'perform' as an efficient minister and have a trail of success behind me. Although He has miraculously supplied me with all my needs, and helped numerous folk through the ministry, there has not been that overflowing blessing out to this dry and thirsty land. When He has clearly dealt with all the impatience and impetuosity and reduced me to nothing, then it will be time for Him to work and to take all the glory.

The second disappointment, since moving out in faith, was quite devastating to me. It was a terrible break in fellowship with some that, over the years, I had come to love more than any others. Just a little of that terrible pain that the Master knew has seared my own heart, as others have failed to understand the way in which one is being taken. What a terrible thing is the pain of being misunderstood by one's brethren and, I suppose, many of His people have suffered this throughout the years and are doing so today. Whereas the Lord was completely innocent, I am sure that both in word and in action I have not behaved in an exemplary fashion; but this I know, that the motives have been pure and that my conscience is clear.

The trial in itself has meant another great step of freedom; freedom from something that I never knew I was in bondage to. One has learned, in a measure, to welcome the things that seem to go wrong as part of the divine plan for our lives, to welcome the suffering as well as the times when we are abounding and there seems not a cloud in our sky. It all began so unexpectedly in one of the local houses where a meeting had been arranged for a visiting speaker.

'*You love something more than Me.*' This was the word the Lord spoke to me as I waited quietly before Him after the meeting. The speaker had expressed views that were terribly radical; he seemed to be saying that he had arrived and that he was now a full-grown son of God, by faith. While I believed in people growing up into what I would call 'sonship' (that is, becoming fully responsible so that God could give unlimited power into their hands), this man did not impress me. He was certainly completely unflappable, but there was a negativeness that worried me, as though it was all likely to drop off in an unguarded moment. There was some truth in what he was saying, of that I was sure; but my Inner Witness would not give any assent to the claims being made. During the question-time I remember taking up some things with him pretty strongly. I discovered that he did not really need forgiveness now as he did not sin and I noticed several in the audience were getting very red under the collar. They were what I would call good orthodox evangelicals. They certainly needed constant cleansing through the blood which Jesus shed for sin, they said, and every night they asked for forgiveness from all that they had done wrong during the day. The speaker said, 'It must be a miserable existence,' and I sould see his point, for these dear people were so obviously *sin-conscious*. They seemed absolutely certain that they were going to continue in sin for as long as they lived; they had accepted defeat, or so it seemed.

The speaker and his contestants were on two ends of a see-saw and my spirit, which would not really witness to either of them, seemed to be sitting in the middle. For the first time I began to realise how self-righteous one can be over being a grovelling sinner in constant need of forgiveness; a sort of false humility—'See what an awful chap I am.' Surely we ought to be able to rise to a greater height than this? Surely we do not need to sin and get forgiveness, sin and get forgiveness, in this interminable way? There must be a higher pathway, I reasoned, and so I cried to God for revelation, that He would answer the problem for me. My wife went on home while I stayed behind to seek more light.

As we talked, I cried out loud, 'God, show me the truth, for I am confused.' He answered, 'You love something more than Me.' What had that got to do with it? I had not fully realised then that, very often, revelation (true light) comes in the school of experience. That is, the matter is not just one of information, it is not academic; but true light does something to a person. The Bible calls it the Light of Life. To have an encounter with the Truth means we are never the same again; it is not a matter of learning something but of literally yielding ground to God. Life from God only comes out of death, for He is the God of resurrection and when everything is in death, or at an end, it is then that He gives His Light, or Life. He is constantly meeting a need and taking us farther along the road.

What was it that I loved more than God? What step had I to take in order that He might shed more precious light along my pathway? As best I knew how, I had offered myself and family, my time and money. Were they not acceptable? As far as I knew everything was at His feet although I realised that I still had a long way to go in the matter of willingly and happily parting with everything at the moment of separation. Everything belonged to Him anyway, for I did not own anything in an ultimate sense. Oh, there was reality beating in my heart, I can tell you; I really did want to know if there was anything holding me back from going right through to the end. Then He told me; it was like a bolt out of the blue, for I had no idea of the nature of my reservation until it was exposed. '*It is the love of your brethren.*' Immediately I was hurt and I knew that a raw spot had been touched. 'Oh no, Lord, not that,' I cried. We had been together undisturbed for over a decade and I had not found what I wanted in any of the denominational churches; now the fellowship of kindred hearts seemed to be everything to me. 'Please, don't touch that or I shall have nothing left.'

The world seemed to be standing still while I counted the cost. Just supposing that God gave me light that my friends would not receive? But that could make no difference to fellowship, I reasoned, for we had always said we were together because we shared the same life, not because we believed the same things. Still the Voice persisted, 'Suppose I give you light that causes your closest Christian friends to turn away from you?' I found myself replying, 'If it's true light, from You, I want it, even if no other man in the whole wide world will receive it.'

This preparedness to 'go it alone', if necessary, gave God the ground to reveal a biblical truth to me, and it did not seem to have any connection with the matter we had been considering. Such are His ways at times, for He knows our *need* and is meeting this continually. He knew my need was to stop striving in my own strength against sin. He wanted to bring me to rest. The light came in the form of two surprising words. . . .

'*You're dead,*' said the Lord.

Immediately a verse from Romans, chapter seven, planted itself firmly in my mind and light came flooding into my soul. 'But if what I would not, that I do . . . *it is no more I that do it*, but sin which dwelleth in me.' It brought instant release and it seemingly had nothing to do with what the man had been preaching; but it was as though a hundredweight of coal had dropped off my back. I was one with John Bunyan as he stood at the Cross and his burden fell away; I was free, chains had fallen away from me in a moment.

There was no great grasp of theological truth; all I knew was that I no longer had to try to be a good Christian. I no longer had to struggle to keep the law of God, for I really was 'in Christ' and when He died I had died and as He was raised so was I; immediately I saw where I had previously missed the way.

At conversion I had been set free from the strain of trying to keep the *Old* Testament law. The Ten Commandments had floored me; that is why I had cast myself on Jesus Christ as my Saviour and proceeded to walk freely in the Spirit, enjoying the liberty of the Christian life. Gradually I had then begun to learn a *New* Testament set of laws which I was equally unable to fulfil; but had been trying to ever since. By my own natural determination I had been trying to fulfil the New Testament imperatives. Instead of perfect freedom, my Christian life had been one of trying because my conscience kept telling me that I ought to be better. There had been an absence of deep rest!

Oh, what an emancipation! I bounded home to my wife; it was now very late and she was in bed. 'I'm dead, I'm dead,' echoed round the bedroom. She obviously wondered what it was all about, for I had never looked so much alive! My wife reminded me that I had been preaching this truth for ten years. What was so different? I tried to explain that now I *knew* I was dead. For years I had been telling myself it was true; but it had not really worked. Now it would be easy to 'reckon' it continually, whatever the circumstances, because I was working from a different foundation.

'I'd like to run down the streets of the town and tell everyone,' I said on waking next morning. We realised together, lying there in bed, that these were exactly the words which Watchman Nee had said when he had the same revelation. Only with him it was Shanghai and it had taken him seven years to see it, but with me it was now eleven years since conversion.

I was free, really free, from my old accusing self and had found a release which was evident to many. It was not long before I was in trouble.

'Don't you realise that you have responsibility?' 'You're so dead, you'll be no use to anybody.' Why was everyone so opposed to this revelation? I did all I could to make it plain, but I did not succeed. Something had happened; that is all I really knew. The strain had gone out of my Christianity and I felt able to relax. For years I had known the cliche, 'Let go, and let God'; but had kept my own hands firmly on the wheel lest there be a smash. Now I was like the co-driver and it was all so different.

It was the loneliest year I have known. Out in the work of God, with my home base feeling that I was off the rails. Several times I got confused by the pressure that was put upon me and tried to explain, but each time the theologians seemed to win the day. They pointed out to me that 'positionally' what I said was true, but that 'experimentally' the old Maurice Smith was still very much alive and they could see plenty of him! The Word of God, I pointed out, used no such terms and the effort of constantly trying to bridge the gap between my position (so called) and my experience had been a heart-breaking business down the years. I said that the 'old me' was dead and that as I continued to walk 'as alive from the dead', then I would less and less fulfil the lusts that were in my flesh. I was not scholar enough to explain to them the difference between my 'old man' that was dead and 'my flesh' which they could see, and anyway, to be truthful, it did not seem that they were very anxious to enjoy what was such a thrill to me!

It was constantly alleged that I had arrived (!) and that I was preaching something called 'sinless perfection', and that very soon I would be living in obvious sin and calling it by less offensive names. But, in fact, sin had become even more obnoxious to me. Could I sin deliberately that grace might abound? God forbid! Or as J. B. Phillips puts it, 'What a ghastly thought!' The whole trouble was that I had seen I was dead, that I had revelation, and I knew that if I quietly accepted what was true of me 'in Christ', then my experience would come trotting along behind in obedience.

'Sin no longer had dominion over me' and there was no need for me to sin at all, as long as I remained where I was. Abiding in the Vine was the place for me (Jesus said, 'I am the vine, you are the branches'), and I decided to stay where I was, to 'walk in the Spirit' and not to 'fulfil the lust of the flesh.' No more trying for me. I saw that the sin I was *accountable* for was when I had been tempted and had yielded, drawn out, if you like, of my resting place in Christ. If I stayed where I was then there was no need for this to happen.

It dawned on me that going on with God was as simple as receiving Him, and that by my previous self-effort, I had removed myself from the realm of Grace—where the ability of God worked for me—back into a realm of law-keeping. I read, and re-read, the book of Galatians and realised that Paul could have written every word of that letter direct to me in the twentieth century. After two thousand years it was completely applicable to my situation, and when he said they were 'foolish Galatians' for getting back to a law-keeping ground, it was as though he said, 'Oh, foolish Maurice Smith.'

In spite of all the opposition from those so dear to me, I sailed through that year at an altitude of several thousand feet. It was wonderful, God was so real to me. There were battles enough; but always this great truth saw me through: 'The battle is not mine, it is the Lord's.' I was at rest.

The group with whom I met had been keeping in step with each other as best we could over the years, and when any individual thought he had received fresh light from God he always shared it openly. But when I briefly testified to my release from the power of sin I was accused of assuming a superior spiritual position. Hadn't we always embraced the doctrine of Romans 6 and 7, which was the truth I was now enjoying? Pressing through from doctrine to experience had again been a costly step, another painful illustration that doctrine by itself does not guarantee fellowship.

This second disappointment after following the call to full-time service had enabled me to enjoy another step of freedom. I had lost the close fellowship of some dear friends for a while but had found out how to live the Christian life without worry.

Whatever people said about my now evading the 'daily working of the Cross', I knew that for the first time in my life I was embracing suffering willingly. Now I wanted to 'take up my Cross' joyfully, instead of putting up with something that God was doing to me. Before I had borne it bravely and put up a good front. Now I found, in real measure, a desire to partake of His sufferings, that I might become a full-grown man or perfected in stature. After so many years I realised that the pathway we have been called to tread is only possible in the strength of Christ. We need to 'know the power of His resurrection' before we can enter into 'the fellowship of His sufferings'.

Why are people so afraid of perfection? Jesus said we should be perfect. I only wish folk were as afraid of imperfection as they are of perfection.

Well, go on; ask it! Have I sinned since that day of mighty revelation? I'm afraid so; but not nearly so much. Instead of trying always not to sin, I now know I need not ever sin again, if I just stay where I am in Christ. The old serpent makes many attempts to draw me out of my resting place, but by the wonderful grace of God we grow wise to his methods, though sometimes we get hurt as we learn. When the enemy has scored a point he makes an awful fuss about it; but we act on the principle of instant confession, instant cleansing and instant restoration. Norman Grubb describes it very well when he likens the business to an infantryman getting in past our line of defence. When the line is pierced he shouts as loud as he can, 'You're *not* dead!' but we know he is wrong. So we quickly throw the infantryman out again. So we live in a world of 'no condemnation' as we walk in the Spirit, as we constantly relax in the Lord Jesus Christ.

. . . . .

Real freedom is freedom from oneself and one's own dictates. I found that Jesus Christ made the all-inclusive bid for freedom when He walked up that hill of Calvary amid jeering and spitting—and He won! Not one selfish thought, not one word that lacked the fulness of love; He had triumphed in whatsoever state He was! Not for Himself but for all men everywhere, right down into the twentieth century, that victory extends, and I have come into the good of it. In spite of a world splitting at the seams, rent with violence and hatred, still His true disciples find His great peace flooding their lives as they learn to rest in Him. They are filled with genuine hope in a situation that, to the trembling hearts around, seems hopeless.

There are more experiences ahead, for the Christian life is one of experience, not of dogma and church ritual. It is a New Life, not a way of life. Nevertheless, the great impression of the steps of freedom I have just related will never leave me; that I know. Freed from the power of an evil spirit; freed from dependence on this world; freed from the worry of trying to keep holy—what next, Lord? I cannot turn back, for 'You have the words of eternal life' and I must follow to the end.

A FINAL WORD OF EXPLANATION

I HAVE been made aware that as this book has been read through, several questions may have arisen concerning my present position. It would be helpful if I could tie up all the ends, but I cannot, for my spiritual history is incomplete. Nevertheless I will do my best to say a few final words about how I feel *now*.

I am wonderfully happy in my faith and have never regretted that momentous step taken by my bedside over thirteen years ago. There is a present rest from striving to be a good Christian and I am enjoying being continually filled with the Holy Spirit as I drink of Jesus.

The group with whom I have been meeting is still progressing although many changes have taken place. I am still with them in spite of some of the revelations which were found to be so devastating. Now many are enjoying the same liberty from the dominion of sin, the same freedom from striving and the same presence of the Holy Spirit that was resisted a while ago. There are problems because of the resistance to changes, but that seems inevitable with progress. There is now a clear conviction that 'we' are not 'it'; and there are constantly increasing opportunities for fellowship with all other believers. We are discovering a oneness which is spiritual and not merely doctrinal or geographical. The Lord is putting more emphasis on informal home meetings, and leading us away from set meetings in special places.

God is obviously working in many different places in many different ways, and I now hesitate to be hasty in my judgment in case I am found to be working against God. However, I am still quite sure that a 'system' is not according to God's full thought but that He wants to run our church life in exactly the same way as our individual lives, that is, on a moment-by-moment basis under the control of the Holy Spirit—not as having been 'taken over' but as we are willing co-operators with every slightest whisper. Where there is a refusal to acknowledge the present working of the Holy Spirit I must admit that it has been difficult to share really full fellowship; not because of any drawing back on my part but because true unity is only produced by, and experienced in, the Spirit. This is as far as I dare go for the moment.

My concern for the unevangelised grows daily, much to the delight of many who have always been aware of my lack in this direction. I am concerned that there shall be a deep work of conviction of sin, both among Christians and those outside the church.

If you start earnestly to seek God, will your experiences be the same as mine? I doubt it, for God has His own unique way of dealing with each one of us, and things may happen to you in quite a different order, and perhaps in a less dramatic way, than they have happened to me. We often hurt ourselves so much because of our resistance to God's workings, but I am convinced also that preparation for our ministry plays its part in the way God handles us.

What more can I say? It has all been worth while and

I feel that perhaps one day I will be asked to write part two; if so, I hope you have been captivated enough by the experiences portrayed within these pages, to come with me on the second half of life's journey.